Bible Interpretations

Seventeenth Series
July 7 – September 29, 1895

*Exodus, Leviticus, Numbers, Deuteronomy,
Joshua & Numbers*

Bible Interpretations

Seventeenth Series

Exodus, Leviticus, Numbers, Deuteronomy, Joshua & Numbers

These Bible Interpretations were published in the Inter-Ocean Newspaper in Chicago, Illinois, during the late 1890's.

By
Emma Curtis Hopkins

President of the Emma Curtis Hopkins Theological Seminary at Chicago, Illinois

WISEWOMAN PRESS

Bible Interpretations: Seventeenth Series

By Emma Curtis Hopkins

© WiseWoman Press 2013

Managing Editor: Michael Terranova

ISBN: 978-0945385-68-4

WiseWoman Press

Vancouver, WA 98665

www.wisewomanpress.com

www.emmacurtishopkins.com

CONTENTS

	Foreword by Rev. Natalie R. Jean	ix
	Introduction by Rev. Michael Terranova	xi
I.	The Bread Of Energy	1
	Exodus 22:1-17	
II.	Grandeur Is Messiahship	9
	Exodus 32:30-35	
III.	Temperance	19
	Leviticus 10:1-9	
IV.	The Alluring Heart Of Man	27
	Numbers 10:29-36	
V.	As A Man Thinketh	37
	Numbers 13:17-23	
VI.	Rock Of Eternal Security	47
	Numbers 31:4-9	
VII.	Something Behind	55
	Deuteronomy 6:3-15	
VIII.	What You See Is What You Get	65
	Joshua 3:5-17	
IX.	Every Man To His Miracle	73
	Joshua 6:8-20	
X.	Every Man To His Harvest	83
	Joshua 14:5-14	
XI.	Every Man To His Refuge	91
	Joshua 20:1-9	
XII.	The Twelve Propositions	99
	Joshua 24:14-25	
XIII.	Review	111
	I Kings 8:56	
	List of Bible Interpretation Series	125

Editors Note

All lessons starting with the Seventh Series of Bible Interpretations are Sunday postings from the Inter-Ocean Newspaper in Chicago, Illinois. Many of the lessons in the following series were retrieved from the International New Thought Association Archives, in Mesa, Arizona by, Rev Joanna Rogers. Many others were retrieved from libraries in Chicago, and the Library of Congress, by Rev. Natalie Jean.

All the lessons follow the Sunday School Lesson Plan published in "Peloubet's International Sunday School Lessons." The passages to be studied are selected by an International Committee of traditional Bible Scholars.

Some of Emma's lessons don't have a title. In these cases the heading will say "Comments and Explanations of the Golden Text," followed by the Bible passages to be studied.

Foreword

By Rev. Natalie R. Jean

I have read many teachings by Emma Curtis Hopkins, but the teachings that touch the very essence of my soul are her Bible Interpretations. There are many books written on the teachings of the Bible, but none can touch the surface of the true messages more than these Bible interpretations. With each word you can feel and see how Spirit spoke through Emma. The mystical interpretations take you on a wonderful journey to Self Realization.

Each passage opens your consciousness to a new awareness of the realities of life. The illusions of life seem to disappear through each interpretation. Emma teaches that we are the key that unlocks the doorway to the light that shines within. She incorporates ideals of other religions into her teachings, in order to understand the commonalities, so that there is a complete understanding of our Oneness. Emma opens our eyes and mind to a better today and exciting future.

Emma Curtis Hopkins, one of the Founders of New Thought teaches us to love ourselves, to speak our Truth, and to focus on our Good. My life has moved in wonderful directions because of her teachings. I know the only thing that can move me in this world is God. May these interpretations guide you to a similar path and may you truly remember that "There Is Good For You and You Ought to Have It."

Introduction

Emma Curtis Hopkins was born in 1849, in Killingsly, Connecticut. She passed on April 8, 1925. Mrs. Hopkins had a marvelous education and could read many of the world's classical texts in their original language. During her extensive studies she was always able to discover the Universal Truths in each of the world's sacred traditions. She quotes from many of these teachings in her writings. As she was a very private person, we know little about her personal life. What we do know has been gleaned from other people or from the archived writings we have been able to discover.

Emma Curtis Hopkins was one of the greatest influences on the New Thought movement in the United States. She taught over 50,000 people the Universal Truth of knowing "God is All there is." She taught many of founders of early New Thought, and in turn these individuals expanded the influence of her teachings. All of her writings encourage the student to enter into a personal relationship with God. She presses us to deny anything except the Truth of this spiritual Presence in every area of our lives. This is the central focus of all her teachings.

The first six series of Bible Interpretations were presented at her seminary in Chicago, Illinois. The remaining Series', probably close to thirty, were printed in the Inter Ocean Newspaper in Chicago. Many of the lessons are no longer available for various reasons. It is the intention of WiseWoman Press to publish as many of these Bible Interpretations as possible. Our hope is that any missing lessons will be found or directed to us.

I am very honored to join the long line of people that have been involved in publishing Emma Curtis Hopkins's Bible Interpretations. Some confusion exists as to the numbering sequence of the lessons. In the early 1920's many of the lessons were published by the Highwatch Fellowship. Inadvertently the first two lessons were omitted from the numbering system. Rev. Joanna Rogers has corrected this mistake by finding the first two lessons and restoring them to their rightful place in the order. Rev. Rogers has been able to find many of the missing lessons at the International New Thought Alliance archives in Mesa, Arizona. Rev. Rogers painstakingly scoured the archives for the missing lessons as well as for Mrs. Hopkins other works. She has published much of what was discovered. WiseWoman Press is now publishing the correctly numbered series of the Bible Interpretations.

In the early 1940's, there was a resurgence of interest in Emma's works. At that time, Highwatch Fellowship began to publish many of her writings, and it was then that *High Mysticism*, her seminal work was published. Previously, the material contained in High Mysticism was only available as individual lessons and was brought together in book form at that time.. Although there were many errors in these first publications and many Bible verses were incorrectly quoted, I am happy to announce that WiseWoman Press is now publishing *High Mysticism* in the a corrected format. This corrected form was scanned faithfully from the original, individual lessons.

The next person to publish some of the Bible Lessons was Rev. Marge Flotron of the Ministry of Truth International in Chicago, Illinois. She published the Bible Lessons as well as many of Emma's other works. By her initiative, Emma's writings were brought to a larger audience when DeVorss & Company, a longtime publisher of Truth Teachings, took on the publication of Emma's key works.

In addition, Dr. Carmelita Trowbridge, founding minister of The Sanctuary of Truth in Alhambra, California, inspired her assistant minister, Rev. Shirley Lawrence, to publish many of Emma's works, including the first three series of Bible Interpretations. Rev. Lawrence created mail order courses for many of these Series. She has graciously passed on any information she had, in order to assure that these works continue to inspire individuals and groups who are called to further study of the teachings of Mrs. Hopkins.

Finally, a very special acknowledgement goes to Rev Natalie Jean, who has worked diligently to retrieve several of Emma's lessons from the Library of Congress, as well as libraries in Chicago. Rev. Jean hand-typed many of the lessons she found on microfilm. Much of what she found is on her website, www.highwatch.net.

It is with a grateful heart that I am able to pass on these wonderful teachings. I have been studying dear Emma's works for fifteen years. I was introduced to her writings by my mentor and teacher, Rev. Marcia Sutton. I have been overjoyed with the results of delving deeply into these Truth Teachings.

In 2004, I wrote a Sacred Covenant entitled "Resurrecting Emma," and created a website, www.emmacurtishopkins.com. The result of creating this covenant and website has brought many of Emma's works into my hands and has deepened my faith in God. As a result of my love for these works, I was led to become a member of Wise-Woman Press and to publish these wonderful teachings. God is Good.

My understanding of Truth from these divinely inspired teachings keeps bringing great Joy, Freedom, and Peace to my life.

Dear reader; It is with an open heart that I offer these works to you, and I know they will touch you as they have touched me. Together we are living in the Truth that God is truly present, and living for and through each of us.

The greatest Truth Emma presented to us is "My Good is my God, Omnipresent, Omnipotent and Omniscient."

Rev. Michael Terranova
WiseWoman Press
Vancouver, Washington, 2010

LESSON I

The Bread Of Energy

Exodus 22:1-17

*"It doth amaze me
A man of such feeble temper should
So get the start of the majestic word,
And bear the palms alone.
Upon what meat doth this our Caesar feed
That he is grown so great?"*
Cassius' speech concerning Julius Caesar

It makes no difference how poor or decrepit or sickly a human being may seem to be; it is to the everlasting honor of the universal energy that it is perpetually offering its own substance to every human being as a reviving bread and quickening elixir ever instant, world without end.

Julius Caesar had epilepsy, he was bald headed, and continually ridiculed by his soldiers, yet he ate of an elixir with some hidden faculty and the ages call him great. Moses was slow of speech, secretly vain, easily discouraged, but he ate of the offered bread and when he said, "I and the Lord thy God, which have brought thee out of the land of Egypt, out of the house of bondage," the people believed that the omnipresent energy itself was speaking to them.

Whenever the people began to lag in their belief that it was the omnipresent Jehovah that was voicing from Moses, all he had to do was to go apart by himself in some mountain place and re-feed himself of the energy. Then they rallied again.

That offered bread Abraham ate sitting in his tent doors at the evening tide on the rolling plains of prehistoric Mamre. By some untaught instinct Lincoln tasted of the never withheld substance; and by the same star-lit touches he broke the bread for millions who had never had instruction in the art of eating the mystic mystery of free life and fearless altar fires.

The hour strikes one, on the sun-sprinkled timepiece of eternity to herald the prophesied one who, though knowing how to taste of the heaven, offered energy of which the great and good of the ages have partaken unknowingly, shall show all men from the least unto the greatest how to feed and re-feed themselves with light and fire and majesty.

"Lo! He cometh. In the volume of the book it is written of him."

Relation of Commandments to Moses

The regular lesson of today's Exodus 22:1-17, it is called the Ten Commandments. They are the language that sprang from the fire of Moses after he had taste of the influence streaming down from the throne place which he had been watching. It is not spoken plainly that Moses knew that he was watching his own divinity point, but all who know how grandly exact all their movements are after they have recognized their own kingly quality are quick to see that it was the "I am" of Moses himself giving down its substance in such a fashion that what its outward lips declared was very commanding.

He did not explain that all people are certain to have the same identical powers when they watch their own "I am," but he did say boldly: *"Thou shalt have no other gods beside me."* The "me" in every one of us is entirely capable of looking out for all our environments and they are so beautiful when left to that rich king on our central throne that all these people with their lame feet and anxious manners are verily that the graven images of fictitious "I am's" which we gladly let get behind us as soon as ever we can when we face the gracious "me."

Moses said *"Thou shalt not make unto thee any graven image, or any likeness of anything that is in heaven above or that is in the earth beneath or that is in the water under the earth."* He meant for us to look so steadfastly unto our own "Me" that our fictitious "me's" would not grave either the divine heavens, the divine earth, the divine waters, with birds killing and tormenting, hatching and brooding each other with fishes spearing and biting and spawning with men cutting and shooting and out-vying themselves and animals.

It is well known nowadays that there are four fictitious "I am's" which we can feed upon, and which make the entirely unread activities of earth and water life. Feeding ourselves on either one of these "I am's" will bring sick people into our sight. They are our graven images. They are our work. Every man must give an account of himself for the work of his "I am's."

Dead Men Are but Graven Images

Every dead man is a graven image created by whoever sees him. Whoever sees anything like Paradise is a maker of graven images through the feeding on stories. The "I am's" that cause us to see misery and decay are the four dispositions through which we view our world.

They are not the Christ Jesus view of earth and sky and sea. The first "I am" to feed upon which gives us stony experiences is the fear of blame and the love of praise. Whoever is trimming his conduct and speech to get away from blame, and managing his tongue and clothing so as to get praise, is able to say that his "I am" is whispering its purpose continually. Hear it whisper, softly but plainly: "I dread rebuke, I am happy in praises." It is very poor fodder, and its images hung over the glorious "me" all around him see no end of misery in heaven above and earth beneath and waters under the earth. From feeding on the proper "Me" we are fearless of evil and unmoved by the good. "There is neither black nor white in Christ Jesus."

The second disposition, which makes stony fare for us and graves magistral over earth and heaven which outdo any farmer's cornfield scarecrows, is our love of the favor and praise and our humiliation at the contempt of the opposite sex. Whoever feeds on glee at the attentions and wilts on despair at the indifference of the opposite sex is eating a stone. He will hang the tatters of feebleness and toothlessness and inanity over the divine "Me" fronting him from every direction. "There is neither male or female in Christ Jesus."

The third disposition which is stony eating for us all is the secret "I am" hunting around and dodging about and paying out money and pushing you into corners in order that I may be some great "some" on this earth. It graves the divine "Me" looking down through heaven and up through earth all over with bitterness. "There is neither high nor low in Christ Jesus."

All Meat of the Divine Me

Now, Moses gives it as a strong peremptory commandment that we must not look through these dispositions. He would have had every man looking back up to the glorious throne of peace whereon his own "Me" is sitting if he had languaged himself exactly right, but as Julius Caesar, with all his masterliness through eating toward his divinity, still retained his bald head and epileptic fits; so Moses did indeed retain his obscurity of language whereby he orders men not to do things they cannot possibly help doing till he more clearly explains where that "Me" is upon which they are to feed and to get the start of hard headed old nature at her wicked contrariness of killing and pounding and drowning and earth-quaking.

There is no use expecting anything but grave images covering the splendor of paradise till we have eaten of the divine "Me." "For I the Lord thy God, am a jealous God." "Eat the dropping energy I will feed your eyes on from looking toward me and you shall then see what I see."

"I show mercy unto thousands of them that keep his commandment of looking unto me alone. The thousands and the thousands of trees and people shall show "Me" to them that look toward "me" and feed in the dropping beauty of my smile. Thou shalt not take my name in vain. Thou shalt not secretly whisper that thy "Me" is thy ambition. For thy "Me" is the king of thy throne."

"Remember the Sabbath day to keep it holy." The Sabbath is the silent "Me" resting forever and moving never. Remember the holy throne.

"Why criest thou aloud? Is there no king in thee? Is thy counselor perished?"

The Lord, the King, the "Me" on my throne never perisheth, but the four stones of which I have eaten are perished at sight of the "Me."

Any One May Enter the Kingdom

Moses commands: *"Thou shalt not kill."* But shall keep killing till I see my "Me" which ordaineth and knoweth not killing. The different "me's" which make up the killing oppositions of nature must keep on with their performances till I see my "Me" and eat of its majestic peaceableness.

"Thou shalt not commit adultery," said Moses. But I must look upon the adulterations as long as I see not and have not and touch not my senses on the holy glory of my own divine "Me."

"Thou shalt not steal," shouts Moses. But I shall steal from your reputation and steal from the reputation of even my own ineffable "Me" till I have altogether fed on sight of it.

"Thou shalt not covet," screams the positive Moses, standing on a rock with two heavy stones in his powerful hands. But I shall wish I had your nobility and I shall wish I had your riches and I shall wish I had your high seat till I have eaten of the bread of energy and majesty and beauty that is now offered me by my own divine "Me" on the high and undefinable throne of myself.

Therefore, it remaineth for the one whose hour is now come to taste and see that the Lord is good and on the bending skies to fling the signals that paradise is in sight. It therefore only remaineth for the greatest among us to be servant to all by drawing aside the coverings that have hidden the face of the wonderful Friend the world has panted to see in the earth. Who among us can leave off eating stones to taste of the bread of the "Me" on his throne? None too feeble to be the prophesied One. None too lowly born to be the prophesied One. None too ignorant and jealous minded and silly to eat of the eternal substance and to be the first one to stop making graven images out of his fictitious "I am's."

> *"It doth amaze me*
>   *A man of such feeble temper should*
> *So get the start of the majestic world.*
>   *Upon what meat hath this great prophet fed."*

The Chicago Inter-Ocean Newspaper, July 7, 1895

LESSON II

Grandeur Is Messiahship

Exodus 32:30-35

Moses was gone a long time in the mountains of silence and the people whom he had led out of Egyptian bondage fell to speaking slightingly of him: "*As for this Moses the man that brought us out of the land of Egypt, we know not what has become of him.*" (Exodus 1:8)

This treachery to Moses was the final blow that liberated his native majesty. As Joseph could not have been anything wonderful if his eleven brothers had not conspired against him, so Moses was never grand till his brother Aaron, his sister Miriam, and all those people whom he had trusted showed out the hidden traits which he had not suspected in their characters.

There are certain Jews who teach that the story of the Messiah's birth and death should be read backward, for in reality the grandeur of man is not born till he has shown how superior he is to the worst that his fellow man can do against him.

Grandeur is Messiah-ship! It shows not till friends turn foes. Then man is born. He must be so stupendous that whatever they say is nothing to him. If they praise him it is nothing. If they slight him it is nothing. If they bury him it is nothing. If they strike him, if they deny his absolutely pure religion, he minds it not. The walls offer no obstruction to his walking through them. They are nothing. Not till such indifference to externals as matter, and also indifference to the mental externals of emotion and ideas is he truly born. "Unto us a son is born, unto us a child is given, and the government, shall be upon his shoulders."

When Paul was in Corinth he fell to financiering and money-making, with the spirit of that city and made his preaching secondary consideration. The government was not on his shoulders. It was on the shoulders of the Corinthian mercantile spirit.

When he was in Athens he went in for eloquent exhibitions of learning exactly like the Athenian spirit. There again government was on their shoulders and not on Paul's thereby showing that Paul a Messiah was not born. When he was in Ephesus he caught the miracle-working spirit and outdid the very Ephesian soothsayers in his excitement; but how great was Paul, if his operations were governed by his environments? How much government is on the shoulders of any man who is great because he has an environment that warms up his greatness but who could not manage an adverse set of circumstances?

The Truest Test of Greatness

And how great is the man who has to strive and exercise and labor with overexertion of mind and body to accomplish the task of conquering his adverse circumstances? He is great to whom large tasks are easy, stupendous situations simple. As a child finds its eyebrows no weight, so the majesty that is born with the government on its shoulder finds the weight of a treacherous world nothing at all.

But how should a man show forth his majesty if the treacherous multitudes did not strike at him? It would be unproved grandeur. When Jesus told them he was no theorizer, he had them thrust their fingers in his sides to see that he was strong and able-bodied with the same stuff that composed the rest of the men, he was no prowling ghost, absent-minded and incapable, but he had carried the cross and the tomb and the slanders of men as slightly as a child carries its eyebrows.

So Moses took the great resistance of two million minds as lightly as his birth of greatness was able. He offered to bear the whole weight of the law of cause and effect. (Exodus 32:30-35)

He made the peoples cause his own cause, and took the one only way to make the law of resistance of no effect. That is, he offered the whole people to the divine majesty on the throne of his own being.

He knew that it was his own "I am" that must be exposed as able to meet the people's crusade against him as he had always known that it was his own "I am" that had started him out on his tour as free man and man freer.

Long before Moses it had been taught that every man ought to fight the battles of life as though a warrior within him were doing the fighting if he wanted to win splendid victories easily. This warrior within is the Messiah in us all alike. When great situations confront us this Messiah is exposing himself as if the situations are easily managed. He is utterly unborn if they are difficult and heart-trying for us. We are only whimpering martyrs while we have heartaches and headaches with carrying the burden of life. The born Messiah does not ache. The government is on his shoulders. Nothing daunts him. Nothing wearies him.

In This Was Moses a Martyr

In so far as Moses was hurt, his majesty was not yet born. In so far as the people took the consequences of their opposition to him, his Messiahship was not exposed. He was martyring himself. And in as far as a man is martyring himself, defending himself, for governing the people; he is not making the people free. They are resisting him, he is resisting them, and the warfare makes trouble and disaster.

Read Exodus 32:35, and see how the people were plagued because Moses stopped short of making their opposition to him entirely naught. "Who shall save me from my sin save he that seeth no sin in me?" And who is great enough to see no sin in me save the "I am" in him that looketh at me? Who is great enough to see no sin in a whole world? His eyes shall melt the enmity of very kings in sinfulness.

The simple practice of healing from sickness by mind depends upon our regarding the sickness as nothing at all — simply nothing. Who is there to whom all sickness is nothing? His name is greatest among good workers.

The simple practice of annulling insanity depends upon regarding it as nothing — nothing at all. Who is great enough to regard all insanity as nothing at all?

To Moses the people's antagonism was great — very great. But he took it and left it as much as his exposure of his "I am" made possible. So they were not free and he was not free. That is, not utterly free, for *"the Lord plagued the people because they made the calf, which Aaron made."* (Verse 35) Aaron had been hypnotized into making the calf, but it was not less plaguing to him than to them. Both hypnotized subject and the hypnotizing public were plagued. For Moses made a great power out of public sentiment as compelling to do the things they don't want to do.

The Weakness of Paul

It is the sign of the greatness of a man when he is not moved by public sentiment, as Paul, influenced by mercantile feeling in Corinth, by learned expositions in Athens by miracle working in Ephesus, being all things to all men, and never himself with the independent government on his own shoulders through ignoring other men's ways. Peter was a different man. When he met a situation he was himself right through it and the situation had to feel him. Aeneas, the cripple, had been waiting eight years for some man to come along who would not fall in with him in his crippledom. Every man, woman, child, had seen him as something stupendous. To Peter it was as easy to hold his own views unmolested by public sentiment or individual notions as it was for Paul to get depressed in Corinth and grow excited in Athens.

"I think I shall be healed some time in the future," said Aeneas. "The future, indeed!" said independent-minded Peter. "Stand up this minute!" And it was after such mind that the government was on Peter's shoulders and not on Aeneas."

And it is after such mind that the "I am" in any man being attended unto fears when accidents and misfortunes crash, and whiffles ground into glee when fortunes and honors besiege us.

Thus the golden text is appropriately chosen, namely, "Little children, keep yourselves from idols." An idol is anything that has the government on its shoulders over us and not we ourselves.

The great silly thing that the Israelites set up was gold. They wanted the gold standard regardless of the "I am" in themselves, which has such an indifference toward differences in values that it makes silver and copper and iron equal in its sight, and whoever catches sight of his own "I am" will soon see that gold has no more value than silver and it is the restoration of selfishness that tries to set it up for a standard. (Exodus 32:4)

The gold and silver and copper and clay and stone entrenchments of all mankind together are nothing — nothing at all — to the man entrenched in his own "Me." It stands out on the earth wherever he walks and his presence is the one with the government on its shoulders.

Fulfillment of Daniel's Vision

Daniel looked forward to this day in which we are flinching under the situations that have the government on their shoulders over us as a company of nations dotting a globe, and with an eye lighted forward from the torch fire of his original "I am" he found somebody holding his or her own among the idols and finally setting up the divine nature in our midst, regardless of the numbers if opponents and the solidity of their entrenchments.

Before this one all inhabitants of earth shall be as nothing (Daniel. 4) and he shall break in pieces the iron, the brass, the clay, the silver, and the gold powers of the solid entrenchments of school and church, and state and society systems which have crowded down some and pushed others up, according to their relation to gold: *"These (calves) be thy gods, O! Israel, which brought thee up."* (Verse 4)

According to the mystery of the orderliness with which these international lessons have come to be related to the life of each individual and nation for which they are written, it would now seem that some other power than our own "I am" had the government over us, but without Moses eye on the "I am" in the exalted region of our own being we are setting ourselves out of the reach of the plagues that belong to us regarding our life burdens as weighty, and our life paths as thorny. The majesty of the Safe One, the secure one within us, standeth forth, is born with the governments on his shoulders insofar as to us nothing hurts, nothing weighs, nothing crowds, nothing depresses.

There is plain evidence of the exposure or the distance from exposure of the Messiah-ship of the warrior within us, by the way the events of our life are regarded this day by us.

Can ye not discern the signs of the times? To the Messiah it is all easy and light. To the Moses it is plague in the half measure. To him that knoweth not that he himself is omnipotent, his circumstances weight him heavy with government over him.

The high and holy One that dwelleth in us each knoweth not of iniquity and knoweth not of excellence. In its indifference is its mightiness. Is it any wonder that the ages have urged indifference as god-like?

"I urged and knew you, oh, king of terrors!" saith the Messiah quality. And over the groans of a world the calming sweetness of Jehovah's eternal smile falls to bless and set free my people. "I take my refuge in thy order, Om."

Chicago Inter-Ocean Newspaper, July 14, 1895

LESSON III

Temperance

Leviticus 10:1-9

The section chose for today's meditation is entitled: "Temperance Lesson." Its text is: *"Do not drink wine nor strong drink thou, nor thy sons with thee."* (Leviticus, 10:9)

It relates how Nadab and Abihu the sons of Aaron, were struck dead for offering incense to the Lord in their own censers and kindling it with strange fire, at which time they were in a state of intoxication. It was a transgression for priests to drink wine within the tabernacle, though they might drink it outside the doors thereof.

It was a transgression for a priest to take his own censer; he must offer incense in the sacred utensil of the sanctuary. It was a transgression for two priests to offer incense together; it should be offered by one alone.

Abihu and Nadab disregarded these regulations and boldly transgressed. Therefore, *"there went out fire from the Lord, and devoured them, and they died before the Lord."* (Leviticus, 10:2)

Now we know that all historic events contain within them spiritual revelations for those who are working their minds along spiritual trainings. Such people do not think wine means an iron pan, they think it means a doctrine.

So they are whirling a universe full of metaphysical phenomena through current literature and through mental zones. They have been quite successful, for even pulpit preachers are beginning to interpret material transactions by spiritual meanings in these latter days.

There are absolute meanings for historic transactions but these absolute meanings seem to the materially engrossed like stones when they touch them, and to the spiritually minded like wandering stars.

Good and Evil Equal

In the absolute sense there is no more good than there is evil, no more life than there is death, no more spirit than there is matter. But to those that are turning matter into spirit and physicals into metaphysicals, matter is to be eaten up entirely by saying that all is spirit and ignoring poor old matter at its faithful tasks of signaling the eternal moveless presence of something that is untouchable by pairs of opposites at their everlasting quarrelings.

For the flesh warreth against the spirit, and the spirit against flesh; as long as a claw or a tooth is left in either of them.

But there is an Indifferent One that commandeth not, running not in a race to whip some antagonists, leaving the field to the combatants, world without end, helping neither side except in one way forever and that only way of help is by destroying them if they recognize its presence.

So Nadab, the free thinker, and Abihu, the bold speaker, both sons, or productions, of illuminated Aaron, turned toward the unidentified Absolute and perished as men, that they might be "It" the absolute.

When the Apostles saw the unidentified Presence they spake in many tongues. The world called them drunk. When Jesus saw the unfighting Presence he heard a divine voice that lifted him as on angels' pinions, but the world said it was thunder; nothing but thunder.

His Ways Mysterious

So when we read this Bible section we are either astonished that the great God was so violent over some incense in two iron pans, and so lenient with Solomon's concubinage, averring with baffled mind that the ways of providence are mysterious, or we say that no man can safely make up a doctrine to suit himself and kindle it with his own eloquence alone, for he surely will find its flaw is its own destruction and his defeat, somewhere along his whirling it before his audiences.

Metaphysically, we do not know the flaw in a doctrine is its dry kindling wood which one touch of divine truth will set on fire. When a man's doctrine is proved a hoax he disappears with the exposure of his flaws. Where now is Mohammed's paradise with its rivers of milk and its plenteous damsels with complexion of honey for those who should follow him?

Where now is the place where infants unbaptized should be thrown if Calvin and Edwards had a flawless doctrine?

Where is the Satan Martin Luther saw? Where is the principle of evil Schopenhauer called God over this universe? Where is that principle of good the transcendentalists set on to fighting evil so victoriously? When one glance of the preachers is turned on him that knoweth neither Good nor evil, being not like unto either, but setting both good and evil into order when they are turned toward him, where are they and where are their fighting premises? "I take my refuge in thy order, Om."

The Bold Abihu

Without doubt it was only the free, bold, and independent Abihu, the speaker, and Nadab, the independent thinker that dared throw the principles of reward and punishment to one side and face the unidentified Om.

They are very bold who find flaws in the religion of their fathers and undertake to swing censers of their own which also have flaws.

For both are destined to kindling wood. Was Martin Luther's doctrine any nearer flawless than his father's before him?

Was George Fox's religion any nearer flawless than his grandfather's before him? Was Christian science any nearer flawless than the church before it, when it substituted evil mentally as a name for the old Satan.

These all and their preachers shall likewise instantaneously depart as Nadab and Abihu, when they are set in sight of Om the unidentified One.

"Aaron held his peace" (Verse 3) when he saw how swiftly a man and his religion disappeared when they were out under the scorching glory of the Absolutely indifferent Presence. And there is nothing that will hurry a man into reasoning as nearly accurate as he possibly can like finding flaws in the religion of fathers. And his reasonings, which are his censers, fired up by his own zeal, for a while intoxicate him with delight, but soon he strikes their flaw and turns his vision higher. Then he is burned and there is only a record of his ridiculousness as now of great Aristides and his imaginary deities who cured him of diseases and directed him in legislation.

Abolishment of Censers

The final abolishment of censers will cause no mourning among the priests who have helped swing them. (Verse 6) But among the people who have believed exactly as their teachers told them and have swung no censers for themselves there is great wailing. (Verse 6)

Those who mean to stick to their censers as it was handed to them and will not step out of the beaten formulas thereof shall still stay on advising all the people not to go drinking strong statements which burn up not only religions but people. (Verse 9)

And these conservative priests are very successful, for the people we do not care to get swung into unattached being are willing to pay for being told over and over that life is more powerful than death if we set the two to go fighting and love is more powerful than hate when we set the two fighting. For this is truth. But for those who have never swung censers on their own account cannot tell the free glory of perishing in the flames of direct sight of the Indifferent One, "before whom all nations of the earth," said Daniel, "are naught, and less than naught," who raineth on the just and the unjust alike, in total indifference to their fights for supremacy.

Breaking Loose from Doctrines

There is no doubt about man perishing as a doctrinal animal and living as unidentified Lord when he boldly breaks loose from old doctrines and swings in ecstatic silliness his own interpretation thereof till it suddenly exposes its modicum of fallacy and, with one final severing from not only his doctrines but himself also, he casts himself into the smokeless flame of the Indifferent Unnamed One that has his abode in our midst.

"If a man thus die shall he live again?" "Yea, verily for I am he that liveth and was dead and alive for evermore."

To have a censer of your own is even now considered a transgression. But who are these that tell me what is a transgression and what is righteousness while the eternal message from my altar fire drops on my head.

"The righteousness of the righteous shall not save him, for all your righteousness is as filthy rags. I, even I am he that redeemeth thee from the last vestiges of those religions under whose banners castes and colors and reelers and steadfast ones keep on and on and on and on."

Let this fire from the Lord fall on me while I proclaim that there is One to know under whose impartial eye there is neither sick nor well, male nor female, learned or unlearned, child, widow, nor merchant be slave, adept nor nabob, and who can make man to see with him, and whosoever seeth that faces that Impartial One first is Jesus Christ to this age.

Chicago Inter-Ocean Newspaper, July 21, 1895

LESSON IV

The Alluring Heart Of Man

Numbers 10:29-36

Manvantara is the day of Brahm, when he is spread like a marching cloud through the universe. Pralaya is the night of Brahm, when he rests like a pillar of fire in moveless majesty. Carlyle says that "difficulty, abnegation, martyrdom, death are allurements that act on the heart of man." That accounts for the charm of opium and its liquid brother. The heart of you is fired to fight so formidable a foe, or enlist in the ranks of such good paying generals. Let the temperance workers describe the terrors of his brother and sister until the cold rivers creep over our sympathetic hearts. Their descriptions are the very battle calls to the young of nations, and at the end of certain days in the fullness of the time of their marching of a mighty increase in the use of these two alluring promises.

This idea of what is most alluring to the heart of man is the subject of today's Bible lesson. All the great authors who sat in solemn council over what was the best offer to make to our children to get them to love their Heavenly Father and great Creator concluded that to offer the severities and rigors of a pilgrimage of life undertaken with the Holy Spirit as a guide would be most appealing. Carlyle is quoted as above, and Ruskin is also quoted, (*Modern Painters,* vol. V). "God wants you to be a Christian not only because it is best for you, but because there is work for you to do in his kingdom; there are multitudes to help, battles to fight, victories to gain." Francis Xavier is raised for dreaming that the Lord of Host the Omnipotent Mercifulness, offered him a vision of his future career as a missionary in his cause. There were shown him weariness, hunger, thirst, sufferings of body, storms to be battled, dangers and death on every hand. He shouted in his sleep: "Yet more, O my God, yet more."

Abnegation Uplifts the Soul

The inference is plain that unless, we can offer more cold and hunger, more rags and death in the service of Brahm than in the service of his great foe, we certainly cannot allure our young ones into his ranks. Our attention is called, therefore, to Moses' invitation to Hobab, the son of Raguel, to come along with the emigrants through the wilderness which they must journey through in reaching the promised land. (Numbers 10:29-36)

"Come thou with us and we will do thee good." And he said, I will not go. And he said, *Leave us*

not, I pray thee, forasmuch as thou knowest how we are to encamp in the wilderness, and thou mayest be unto us instead of eyes."

Hobab himself belonged to one of the powerful tribes who covered in their wells and harassed travelers through the deserts, and so he would be a useful ally. At the notion that he could be of service to the Israelites in their perilous travel toward Canaan, Hobab, the son of Raguel, consented to accompany them.

This is very adroit and plausible reasoning which makes me want your company, because I can serve you or you can serve me, and puts it as holy motive, but it is not the divine battle call and let us not try to plaster over the shining pillar of fire within us by any such idea.

Did the pillar of fire by night and the cloud by day, which symbolized the eternal watch of our own soul within us, promise anything, or ask any help? Was not its whole argument contained in its being what it was and letting men do as they pleased?

What caused Moses to want Hobab's help? Fear of the tribes of the desert. Why did he not keep the eyes of his heart in that smokeless fire and that topless cloud instead of steering them toward the famines and droughts and swords of wilderness? On the same plan that we organize into hands and brotherhoods and companies now for the purpose of fighting and evading enemies in our earthly pilgrimage from the spot where we are to the happy spot we are trying to arrive.

In supreme moments of knowledge of the soul man has always told a different story from what he was told when he has halfway forgotten that his soul in its supernal majesty is self-sufficient: "Let each man have himself to his friend. Let him lean on no companion. Let him walk with no comrade."

It was in the supremest moment of Jesus that "they all forsook him and fled." It was in the first sun of the day of his greatness that Joseph's brethren sold him. It was in the most splendid moment of Moses that he had no helper near the Red Sea path of his journey save the all-sufficient brilliancy of his own soul. It was Esther's crowning beauty that when she touched the divine Helper her people had no faith in her. She was alone with her own limpid, shining soul.

Let women and men bind themselves into companies and tie themselves into knots of regiments and battalions to fight the armed foes of life's desert journey; as for me, let me stand up alone with the omnipotent friendship and irresistible integrity of my unsoliciting fearless soul, and see what it is capable of doing, single-handed and unassisted. Then only shall I be a competent witness of its all-sufficingness, or its non-efficiency.

How much more majestic was this Moses, when standing on the brink of eternity, with

2,000,000 fugitive slaves in his charge, he saw only his soul, and with a loud voice he cried, "The Lord shall fight for you and ye shall hold your peace," than when he is here subtly persuading an alliance of a son of the powers of this world.

Was there not sufficient charm in the marching Brahm? Was there not gladness enough in the still Jehovah, to hold Hobab to the side of Moses?

Then, let him go home to the styes of the foe. The shining soul was comradeship and alliance. Here was one of the tests of great Moses. Did he ever find a Jesus Christ coaxing somebody to help pilot him through the desert wilderness of life, or assist him in meeting the Satan of all his world's conjuring up?

Abraham Lincoln's Influence

Who fires the heart with the most love and awe? Abraham Lincoln, the lonely lad of the cabin, without money and without patron, touching by some soul-taught turn to the altar spark of irresistible God, or the son of a multi-millionaire prancing in epaulettes on a Governor's staff with his pampered comrades beside him?

> *"Speak! Victory, who are life's heroes?*
> *Pilate or Christ?"*

What kind of a religious life must of necessity grow out of such a change of policy on the part of the so-called leader of a people? Must it not be that in common times and ordinary doings we are to get hold of all the strings of assistance that present themselves, but on great occasions we are to lean on the omnipotent whose unfailing presence among us none disputes?

On ordinary days sand the sugar because other growers do it, join a union because it is polite, but when calamity has brooded herself as a result, rise to the heights of calling on the supreme Jehovah, almighty one alone!

Who hath shown us a nation of people whose God is the Lord? That is, where are the men who have joined no rings, tied up, with no combines, identified themselves with no firms, but with steadfast eye on the spreading daylight of their own inner spirit have preached no dangers, to lure in followers and secure in the self-sustaining greatness of the soul in all men, have preached no land of plenty and health to bait them on with, but let their own light do its own appealing, offset the Hobab sons of this world to retire to wherever they would?

How can we tell what the Jesus would have been if Moses had not preached good fortune as an inducement to follow the Lord, and, falling with that bait, take Carlyle's more promising allurement, namely, "difficulty, abnegation, martyrdom, and possible death?"

How can we tell what a religion might have been the precedent of Jesus if cold and hunger for one bait, and milk and honey for the other bait, thrown out to the ever-succeeding Hobabs sons of

Raguels, had not been the Mosaic policy generation in and generation out?

Harping on Compromises

Is there no intrinsic attractiveness in the Brahm glory itself? Is there nothing heart drawing in the calm splendor of the everlasting pillar of fire by night and cloud by day, assuring man by its eternal nearness that it is sufficient, day by day, for meeting the Midianites of the world wilderness, as well as Pharaoh and the Red Sea?

The sons of Raguel are all these people on our globe. Is there anybody with the eyes of his heart set so fearlessly in the Brahm fire, burning forever, nearer than his breath, that he can tell them of its eternal sufficiency? Must our learned authors and sacred preachers still harping on the Moses compromise, or half way position of baiting our Johns and our Lucys toward Jehovah with rags and famine, or health and long life?

Wist we not that the sons of Raguel have the living flame in their own hearts, and to point toward it as equal to sustaining itself forever in them, is sufficient to make all the wilderness and the garden one and the same to them since Jehovah, their fire is enough?

How do we know what kind of a world would be greeting our eyes if we had not been taught to be brave on a terrible journey called life? Did we ever think what kind of a people we ourselves might now be had we been taught of Jehovah Jesus, the light by night and the shelter by day, and he had been shown as our sufficiency, needing no careful trading on our part to keep in with the Hobabs and Raguels lest we lose our bread and our roof-trees?

Who said that the journey of life is fraught with dangers? *"For as I live,"* saith the Lord, *"I know the thoughts that I think toward you; thoughts of peace and not of evil."* And: *"Why have ye made the heart of the righteous sad whom I have not made sad?"* saith the Lord.

Might not Hobab, married as he was into the very family of Moses, being as commentators discover not "father-in-law," but brother-in-law, have himself seen something in the eternal pillar worthy of his adoring obeisance, had not Moses put his own wary preachings before his face?

Incessant Praying Needed

After that Moses had to spur up the ark with incessant prayings else the very things he had himself suggested should come upon them all.

And it came to pass when the ark set forward that Moses said Rise up Lord and let thine enemies be scattered, and let them that hate thee flee before thee.

And when arrested he said: *Return O Lord, unto the many thousands of Israel.* (Verses 35, 36)

Go forward and return. This is the day with its stopless march, and nigh with its moveless glory. This is breath forward and breath inward. This is the native way of Brahm, with nobody urging him on and nobody responsible for his Majesty.

Wherever men have to "treat" the ark of the Lord to charge it up with power you may know they have been "doing in Rome as the Romans do," or, in other words, finding it necessary to use the crutches of comradeship to help them be happy and successful. With one it is wife, with another it is son, with another it is a friend, or father, or mother, or syndicate, or union, or firm that cannot be dispensed with. "The ark of the Lord" is our hope in the Lord. Our hope in the eternal Brahm needs no sacred fanning up with prayings while the Lord himself is visible as the smokeless flame of an unfailing, competent presence whom to see is to be satisfied with.

His own way of doing is its own appeal. Where is he that is satisfied enough with his sight of everlasting one as his shelter by day and his inspiration by night so that he leaneth on no companion, he asketh no comradeship? He is the father of the "new nation that shall spring up in a day." "For the Lord hath set the solitary in earth's great family," but he acteth not like this Moses.

Chicago Inter-Ocean Newspaper, July 28, 1895

LESSON V

As A Man Thinketh

Numbers 13:17-23

Moses sent out twelve spies to search the promised land. Ten of those spies brought back a report of the great size of the inhabitants of that land and the fierceness against strangers. Two of the spies reported that the land was fertile and worth entering, the inhabitants were pregnable, and it being the land of the Lord's promise unto them it was their duty to go forward and possess it.

The result of the report of the ten spies was that the 2,000,000 Israelites refused to go and take possession. They rebelled against Moses who had got them out of Egyptian bondage only to deliver them into the teeth of Canaanite giants.

As Bible history registers, the result of this rebellion was that the ten spies who made a dark report were smitten with plague and dropped out of sight. Every person over twenty years of age stepped into his grave before the promised land was entered. Only the two faithful spies, Caleb and Joshua, of all the adult Jews, touched the grasslands and vineyards of beauteous Canaan. Even Moses could only behold it from afar and all this because of heeding the ten dark saying of their own servants.

Experts on languages now report to us that in our own day there are five times as many words to express evil as to express good in the sum total of words of all languages. If a child has a fever there are five fears to one encouragement talked over in that house. If a woman has deafness, there are ten apples called doctors, to two spies called cranks, pronouncing on its incurability. And as in the case of these Jews of 1490 B.C., the majority have the floor, and she keeps her deafness plus the discouragement and hopelessness of forty years of travel in the wilderness ahead of her.

Lessons Written in Exalted Moments

For Bible segments were but object lessons written in exalted moments by the poets of old Israel, who, as majestic in diction as Shakespeare, and as entranced as the seer of Patmos, lifted up some hints to man concerning his own central soul fire and its twelve powers of action.

Whether it is true that any monkey ever used a live cat's paw to pull chestnuts out of the fire with or not, the application is a fact of daily occurrence. Without doubt every reader of these lines has been both the user and the used on more than one occasion. So whether any veritable Moses ever led 2,000,000 liberated serfs through a wilderness during forty years, searching after a glorious land out of sight, but close at hand, yet the materialists will continue to see always and forever only that there are five false reports on life, health and destiny to every one true report, and if we attend to them we lie down in the sands of unsuccessful endeavor, each one with Tulliver's last remarks on his record, expressed or unexpressed: "The world has been too many for me."

The matchless genius of sacred song and story is in that they always apply to every individual who reads them, and they apply to every tribe and every church and age as exactly as if printed in the day they were read. Thus, this day's set of texts, running from Numbers 13:17-23, touches on my coming weeks' experience and your coming weeks' experience, and we may side in with the ten signs of evil about to salute us or we may agree with the two principles of success also about to rise up within us.

As A Man Thinketh in His Heart

Let us know that the messages of evil may be our own mental cogitations, and the two principles of good may be just two simple denials and affirmations brought out by the new Christian theology and remembered in secret by us, yet the future of our career shall hinge on our dealing with them, even if we never speak a loud word.

For, be it known unto the lands and the seas of earth with all the inhabitants thereof that every man works out his own destiny in the secret arena of his own mind-plane before he puts it on the bank stocks and baldness of his business coiffure.

Solomon in the exaltation of writing things which he could not remember to practice sang, *"As he thinketh in his heart, so is he."* (Prov. 23:7) Shakespeare, in the upland wisdoms that often blew their stopless winds through his fingers wrote: "But I, unless I think what has happened is an evil, am not injured, and it is in my power not to think so."

And, be it known unto the city authorities of every land and the rulers of every nation, that there be some among the people who know how to swing the bones and sinews of their invisible thoughts to carry those rulers wither they will and they shall topple to the secret suggestions as supinely as poor Prendergast, who was hanged for somebody else's idea.

In a certain city the school board did not want to employ one particular teacher, but her friend a bright woman with mental muscles sat near them, and over and over repeated the words, "You want the teacher, you want the teacher, and as obediently as trained schoolboys, those majestic men hired the teacher. Perhaps they knew Greek roots, perhaps they could calculate angles and curves, but, as said the sage of Palestine, "One thing thou lackest." O Daniels, come to judgment, namely, a little score from the music of Schopenhauer and Collier.

In the Ghostly Realm Called Mind

Another marched the silent troops of thought that had camped in untrained hosts on the tented fields of her mind to the bugle call of one rallying sentence, and a certain judge was as powerless as a baby to decide the case against her estates. The hand-organ man, whose dirty fingers catch your pennies, has as much force and efficiency on that ghostly territory called mind as the President of our Republic or the Prince of Wales or the Czar of all the Russias.

The Jews discovered Canaan, Columbus discovered America, but the uncanny zones of thought where the men kings wander, who hath set foot on them?

"Who hath believed our report, and to whom is the arm of the Lord revealed?"

There are those among us who have found that when we arrive in this mind region we may drop thoughts and attend to one great Fact, which is as far out of the reach of mind as the school woman's secret decree was above the school board's aversion to the teacher she wanted to put in, but this lesson of Moses and the twelve spies is intended to deal with activities and destinies on the mind-plane, so we will speak on that line. You will remember that last Sunday's lesson showed Moses as representing any man who has seen the unearthly grandeur of his own divine soul as its eternal task of guiding him into paths of safety and strength. It showed that the Moses man found out that there is one unalterable Fact in space which nothing can take from or add to. That fact was his own "I am."

The One Unalterable Fact

He could not be taken from or added to He himself was the Fact. It had such an effect on the commonplace Moses, timid, stuttering, vanity tinctured, that it made him grand beyond description. On the desert wastes ahead of the wandering Jews was dropped each night a banner of fire to show which way to pitch their folded tents as day's march nearer home. On the eternal sands under the steady glare of Asiatic suns day by day the somber shadow of a mountain raise ever, pointed its cooling streamers toward Canaan, the land whither the exiles hastened. This man was an emblem of the uprisen "I AM" of Moses.

But on a day Moses saluted a great fear. This fear caused him to ask Hobab to go with him as a guide through the wilderness. And now his own fear has multiplied itself by ten. And his own fear ramifies from the ten agents, to whom he has deputed it, through the breasts of two million people, minus Caleb and Joshua, the two silent forces within Moses own heart which are all that can now keep the guiding pillar anywhere in sight as the emblem of the power of the soul in the deserts of human transactions and the Red Seas of misfortune. Last Sunday's lesson showed that by urging

Hobab to go with him to help him, Moses taught himself a different policy for every-day transactions from what he used on great occasions. On great occasions he would stand alone with the Almighty, and let its unconquerable majesty take absolute care of him. On this policy he is able to drive the Red Seas back and draw manna from heaven without leaning on Hobab or any other man. But when the humdrum of daily marching is going on, he is afraid of the Hittites, the Amelikites, the Jebusites and the rest of the "ites," and begs Hobab to help him, while yet the shadowy pillar smiles in sight with tender reassurance.

The Defect in Moses Example

By these compromises he has led off millions of men in later ages, who through gratitude for his greatness at the scene of the Red Sea, have unthinkingly followed him as a leader in conduct on daily half measures.

Out a such leadership has grown a civilization whose merchants sand the sugar six days in the week because of other grocers doing so, fearing to compete in the forty years business of wilderness with other grocers, who make money out of sand, and on the seventh day bless the mighty God of Abraham, Isaac, and Jacob, who by his high arm and outstretched hand carried men through deeper dangers than grocers unions.

Last Sunday's lesson was meant, so far as the profounder teachings could be expressed, to show that Moses set the fashion 3,385 years ago of appealing to what Carlyle declares is the most sensitive chord in man's nature, to make converts with. That is, he appealed to Hobab's love of danger. As this state of affairs mentioned in today's Bible segment is the straight outcome of last Sunday's record on saluting fear on common days but rousing to fearlessness on great occasions, we will mention what Carlyle and modern reformers agree is the most sly way of converting our young ones to love of the glistening wonder burning at their own hearts, which is their immortal soul never born of flesh by father and mother and never mixed up with earthly transactions.

The Fascination of Danger

"Difficulty, abnegation, martyrdom, death, are the allurements that act on the heart of man." — Carlyle. So Moses was temporizing a little, working on Hobab's danger-chord, but there was no danger in sight, and none en route, for the pillar of the Lord went forward, and the glory of the Lord went rearward, and the angels of Jehovah encamped round about them day and night. At first Moses tried to allure Hobab with good fortune, but though that bait might work with some, it did not work with Hobab.

How do we know what the Jews might have been, and what example they might have set us, if their leader Moses had not preached good fortune as an inducement to follow Jehovah, and falling in that bait, taken Carlyle's more promising allurement, namely difficulty, abnegation, martyrdom, possibly death?

Now, this is all on the plane of mind and its outcomes. "Salute no man by the way," said Jesus. Having fixed your eye on the great fact in the universe, that must be enough for you. If you salute a Hobab for assistance, you must salute ten others who can do more with your affairs than Hobab.

Did Hobab take the place of eyes, as Moses hoped? Alas! No. Forty years he kept them roaming around and around, but never reaching Canaan. "Cursed be he that leaneth on the arm of flesh." Lean thou on the omnipotent "I AM" within thee that spreadeth its irresistible defenses withersoever thy pilgrimage leadeth.

The Wisdom Words of the Lesson

This lesson finds Moses and all the Jews just at the verge of forty years with nothing but the memory of a glorious miracle to encourage them and the reassuring voices of the two undying principles burning at Moses own heart altar, represented by Caleb and Joshua, who would not see defeat and death though ten other voices said there was defeat and death, but since Moses was leader, and could listen to his ten fears or go on without saluting them, these two must live as divine voices have mostly lived in the fastness of silent but omnipotent minority.

Applying this lesson home to our standing ground of this week, we may yield to the ten descriptions of our own disadvantages (verse 33) or rouse to our two sacred, undying wisdom words, the first of which is for every one of us, be we card driver or Czar. There is no failure possible to me, for, second, I am the Omnipotent, unswerving One.

Chicago Inter-Ocean Newspaper, August 4, 1895

LESSON VI

Rock Of Eternal Security

Numbers 31:4-9

It is clear that if the one woman with a silent knowledge of what a silently whispered phrase would do could influence a whole school board to hire a teacher they did not want, it is possible, eventually, for the shoe-black by the same occult operation to rule over the actions of the Czar of all the Russias.

It is clear then that new kings on this globe are to be the psychologists, and not the lineal descendants of the Prince of Wales or President Cleveland. These two prominent brothers in genius must certainly flee to some rock of protection more secure than titled thrones in the days when the street-cleaner and the valet know their vested rights on the ghostly territory of thought.

There is a rock for man to stand on which is his sure protection from the psychologist's energies. But while any thinks he himself has more right to life and knowledge than the lackey who tends him, his feet are not on the rock, and he must swing the bones and sinews of his secret thoughts on the common fighting ground with other thinkers, only to get worsted in some off-guard moment.

"For the fox must sleep sometimes;
The wild deer must rest."

The rock of safety is uncognized of social distinctions. The rock of safety does not know that Prince George is of the royal house of Henry VIII. It does not know that you have manufactured a gun capable of shooting down more heads per minute than Colt or Krupp. It knows only itself, and only those who know it are safe on it from the surges of high and low, rich and poor, male and female.

Founded On the Rock

Whosoever feels the need of using his thoughts over and over in order to protect himself from the other thoughts that are flying around his head is not on the rock. Yet the learned school board were not on the rock, for they did what was against their judgment. The judge on the bench was not on the rock, for he decided the case *nolens volens* (willing or unwilling). Many a preacher in his pulpit is now voicing some unlistening parishioner's secret orders, so he is not on the rock.

Jesus of Nazareth must have been on the rock, for while great Pilate and the glistening swords of splendid Rome were pointing their threats at him he said: *"Thou couldst have no power at all, except it were given thee from above."*

He said that he himself was from above, and thus he himself let them use their paste-board vigors against the rock of his eternal security.

The Bible lessons in use by the civilized world (so-called) have been latterly very much like trumpet calls to all mankind to get on the rock place, where man shall be as secure from thoughts as from microbes.

These lessons have taught that people who are seeking truth are on the mind plane where thoughts are things and thoughts are kings. These lessons have taught that Moses is paraded on the everlasting canvas of sacred writ to show the law of cause and effect, which in our day is called Karma. These past lessons have shown that Jesus of Nazareth was paraded on the everlasting canvas of sacred writ to show man absolute escape from Karma. He is shown as so on fire with the absolute that he was and is the absolute. His name and the Father are one name. *"In that day ye shall pray unto the Father in my name."* *"There is none other name given whereby man can be saved."* *"Look unto me and be ye saved."* There is nothing for man to be saved from except Karma. And that is the law of cause and effect. This law itself is only a delusion of man started up on the uncanny tenting grounds of his mind.

Silent Treatment of the Prophets

But the simple denial of Karma does not rid a man of the consequences of his own ghosts, or, rather, his own past thoughts. Look at those miserable mentalists who have been working at denials till their heads shake with palsy and their teeth have long since departed, who could not read a page without pebbled glass assistants.

Was there ever a denial more sweepingly powerful than Daniel's? Yet war and famine and slavery are still kings, because the serfs and the bootblacks have not heard of their rock place safer than denial of famine.

It was under a three and one-half years' course of silent treatment by Daniel, B.C. 570, that, Nebuchadnezzar cried out: "All the inhabitants of the earth are reputed as nothing." It was under the scientific statement that there is only God that Isaiah exclaimed: "Behold the nations are as a drop of a bucket, and are counted as small dust of the balance." "All nations before him are as nothing; and they are counted to him as less than nothing." Yet the earth is still swinging, because denials are not the rock. This man was talking of seeing from the God point of view. He spoke truth. God is too pure to behold iniquity, therefore whoso seeth iniquity it's his own fancy and not true sight.

"Keep your eye fixed on the eternal and your intellect will grow," said Emerson.

"Does this mean our eyeballs lifted up and back at the starting point of our career?" If you have got no farther than eyeballs, up with them, you that would grow. But if you have got to where you can see the eternal I AM in space with a finer set of eyes, use that finer set and see finer issues. It is not customary for those who use the finer set of eyes to quarrel with the eyeballs crowd. But let it be distinctly understood that he who seeth the eternal of which Emerson was speaking is as safe from the snares of secret service and the arrows of silent ignorance as the eternal itself.

There is one I AM in space. Nothing can be added to or taken from that I AM. When I see that I AM I am that I AM, and nothing can be added to or taken from me. This is the science of Christ Jesus.

Lesson of Doing the Best

Today's Bible lesson tells of the two sets of seers. The eyeball seers and the finer seers. Even those who only lifted high the pupils of their eyes got cured of their hurts. If a man does the best he can, he will get better than his best. Who could have thought that these Karma bitten Jews would have got so well cured of their bites by simply casting up the pupils of their eyes? Who would have thought that Moses and Caleb and Joshua could have got cured of their biting belief in the wickedness of neighbors by seeing that the symbol which they lifted up foretold another symbol yet to come? (Numbers 31:4-9)

It was a great thing to get cured of the bites of Arabian snakes, but it was just as great a thing for

Moses to get cured of seeing his neighbors as such paralyzing sinners. He had a great belief in the wickedness of man, but he had another belief fighting it, called forgiveness of sin.

We now have a set of people who work on the Moses plan of calling their neighbors wicked sinners and working their minds up to a flaming point of agony concerning their souls' safety from a future of burning lake, and there at the agony point, handling them the belief in forgiveness.

Now, this is the calomel (purgative) heroics which must be used by those whose eyes are set first on wicked man and then on holy God, but it is not the Christ Jesus way of looking at man, and let us not hide the beauty of his presence by such double-eyed dogmas.

"Neither hath this man sinned, nor his parents." "Do not think that I will condemn you." "I came not to condemn the world."

The golden text of today's lesson tells what the lifting up of Jesus symbolizes. *"As Moses lifted up the serpent in the wilderness, even so must the Son of Man be lifted up."* The serpent has always been the symbol of healing. Its mystery is its glory. The mystery of seeing the I AM in space and seeing nothing else was known to Jesus of Nazareth.

Visions of Jesus and John

He was not a two-eyed dogmatist, seeing the wickedness of men and the goodness of God. His eye was single, therefore his whole body was full of have got no farther than eyeballs, up with them, you that would grow. But if you have got to where you can see the eternal I AM in space with a finer set of eyes, use that finer set and see finer issues. It is not customary for those who use the finer set of eyes to quarrel with the eyeballs crowd. But let it be distinctly understood that he who seeth the eternal of which Emerson was speaking is as safe from the snares of secret service and the arrows of silent ignorance as the eternal itself.

There is one I AM in space. Nothing can be added to or taken from that I AM. When I see that I AM I am that I AM, and nothing can be added to or taken from me. This is the science of Christ Jesus.

Lesson of Doing the Best

Today's Bible lesson tells of the two sets of seers. The eyeball seers and the finer seers. Even those who only lifted high the pupils of their eyes got cured of their hurts. If a man does the best he can, he will get better than his best. Who could have thought that these Karma bitten Jews would have got so well cured of their bites by simply casting up the pupils of their eyes? Who would have thought that Moses and Caleb and Joshua could have got cured of their biting belief in the wickedness of neighbors by seeing that the symbol which they lifted up foretold another symbol yet to come? (Numbers 31:4-9)

It was a great thing to get cured of the bites of Arabian snakes, but it was just as great a thing for

Moses to get cured of seeing his neighbors as such paralyzing sinners. He had a great belief in the wickedness of man, but he had another belief fighting it, called forgiveness of sin.

We now have a set of people who work on the Moses plan of calling their neighbors wicked sinners and working their minds up to a flaming point of agony concerning their souls' safety from a future of burning lake, and there at the agony point, handling them the belief in forgiveness.

Now, this is the calomel (purgative) heroics which must be used by those whose eyes are set first on wicked man and then on holy God, but it is not the Christ Jesus way of looking at man, and let us not hide the beauty of his presence by such double-eyed dogmas.

"Neither hath this man sinned, nor his parents." "Do not think that I will condemn you." "I came not to condemn the world."

The golden text of today's lesson tells what the lifting up of Jesus symbolizes. *"As Moses lifted up the serpent in the wilderness, even so must the Son of Man be lifted up."* The serpent has always been the symbol of healing. Its mystery is its glory. The mystery of seeing the I AM in space and seeing nothing else was known to Jesus of Nazareth.

Visions of Jesus and John

He was not a two-eyed dogmatist, seeing the wickedness of men and the goodness of God. His eye was single, therefore his whole body was full of

John on Patmos saw our day and cried, *"Who shall be able to stand?"* And Jesus saw our day and said, *"I, if I be lifted up, will draw all men unto me."*

Chicago Inter-Ocean Newspaper, August 11, 1895

light. His eye was on the Eternal till he was all of it. So, in time, whosoever should look unto him, should receive better than he asked, exactly as the Jews got clean bodily healing by looking with expectant eyeballs, and Moses got clean healing of his belief in the dreadful naughtiness of the Hebrew children. There is no limit to the healing power of the I AM, whether it is placed, before me as a symbol for my eyes to stare at as the pious Russians gaze at the pictured God in their churches, or as the living man nailed to the cross, which the pious Americans stare at with their minds, or as the undescribable presence forever near, knowing neither of sin nor forgiveness of sin, the changeless and eternal Original. David sang of these Israelites that they limited the Holy One, because they judged and operated by their physical eyeballs; he prided himself on seeing with his mind's eye what was going on. But, even so, this mental acumen did not keep him from setting Uriah in the forefront of the battle for unmentionable reasons.

There is a rock of security for the materially eyed which can heal them of all the snake bites of cause and effect, and there is a rock of safety for the mentally eyed which can heal them of the snake bites of thoughts, and from that rock the lineal descendants of Victoria and of the school boards, and the mayors and judges, must hide, for kings are abroad on the thought planes who are more sinewy than they.

LESSON VII

Something Behind

Deuteronomy 6:3-15

Hugh Black wrote: "It is a fearful thing to be God's favorite. To be chosen of God is a terror." He adds that it is also a "glory" to be a favorite of God.

On the principle of self-projectivity, which is now being demonstrated, that being of whom Mr. Black is talking, is but a projection in space of somebody's fancy. There is in reality no such dangerous character.

Man can see his own interior concepts formulate on the cosmic mirror of surrounding space. If anybody will name a character who never existed he may see a bodiment of that character after a while.

Mr. Hudson, author of "Psychic Phenomena," could call up an imaginary sister on the gloomy ethers of this abyss we call our breath; and she would seem as real as though she had ever lived. So also he could project a brother on the uncanny canvas of this our atmosphere, who could walk and talk as well as Martin Luther's Satan, or Aristides Minerva, or the "medium's" Indian chief.

"We never get outside ourselves," is the common verdict of all the clear-headed unbiased investigators of life in all ages. Thus it stands to reason that I shall be dealt with by the beings of my own projections.

"Till the stars are old,
  And the sun is cold."

For the creative germ eternally dwells in me. And thus it stands to reason that the secret of forty years wandering in the deserts of ignorance practiced by faithful Moses, 1450 B.C., lay in his own creative tendency.

The God of Moses

He imagined a God almost identical with Mr. Black's. This projected reformer was often very unreasonable, expecting the most superhuman faith in the kindness in order to be able to exercise any kindness, then again, disregarding their faith or doubt he helped them and fed them like an indulgent mother.

These differences of dealing all followed Moses' inward concepts so directly that a Jewish writer declared, when addressing this hypothetic operator: "With merciful thou wilt show thyself merciful, and with froward (perverse) thou wilt be froward."

The demand is, then, for an example of what would be the lot of a man who should cease covering the face of the cosmic ethers with imaginations. Has there ever been a man bold enough to stop creating a god and a fiend, either, with separated bodies or all in one? Has there ever been a man who let be what is and found out what Is is? There is no doubt about our perpetually meeting our own inner promptings. Is there anybody who has ever stopped inwardly prompting things and gazed upon what was not prompted?

There is a cult of prompters hailing now from the Asiatic land of beggary who are teaching us with careful analysis about vampires, ghouls, demons, jinns, and the battle of the devas and Asuras. Let one of us listen with credulous mind and soon we see some of these classified fabrications. If we have agreed in the depths of our hearts that we will keep up a lingo of good words to ward off demons and devas we find ourselves worn to threads with the harassing demands of our agreement, for the instant we stop the protecting power in the formulas of words only, so far as we project protecting power into them, we shall rest from our arduous labors of whirling formulas and investing them with powers they do not need.

That Which is Born in Us

Is there any great "I Know" in the universe, whom we could get acquainted with and find out something better to be employing our native energy with, than supposing things about nothing? Is there not something that is what it is, and does what it does irrespective of our say so's? Might we not get acquainted with it and cease from being such endless repetitions of our neighbors?

We talk of the influence of early associations on our children, and attribute to those temporal experiences all their after life. Is there not something that each child is, which no influence can alter? How much of what he seems to be is made up of our fabricated notions of him? May he not be hidden from us by our notions of him as completely as the true "I Know," and the indwelling It is, which no home influences can interfere with while the stars revolve, and no saloon can tempt forever, and forever?

Mr. T. H. Darlow writes for the children of this world that "God's unfinished work is a wonderful fragment, full of hint and hope of what he meant to be." But Moses said that God had finished his work once and was so well pleased with it, that he pronounced it "very good." Which great fabricator of descriptions is correct?

Today's Bible lesson says, that if I go after any of the gods of the people round about us, that Moses' God will get so angry, that he will destroy me off the face of the earth. (Deuteronomy, 6:3-15)

But is Moses' God the real god? Is the real God anything at all like the various descriptions of Him which my neighbors have gyrated around me since I first met them?

The Something Which Lies Behind

Is there one description of the I AM that is grateful to my waiting ears? What may there not be hidden behind those airs, thick with the whirring tales of falsity, which the generations have pasted up?

Walt Whitman saw that there was "something behind; something behind." His poetry was written with every faculty reaching toward the "something behind" that the people talked of.

Did anybody ever touch that "something behind" and free from the carking (burdensome) dominion of conditions? Was anybody ever master of his environments, and not they of him? Was anybody ever independent of money and books and friendships and death and faintness and fame and strength? Was anybody ever acquainted with the unchangeable "I know?"

The international textbook says that "wars open the doors of nations and conquests protect our missionaries." May it not be possible that those missionaries are taking along a fabricated god, if he has to slay men and starve children before he can effect his purposes?

There is something within every born creature that knows that while the panorama of warfare is spreading itself before us we do not know the absolute and eternal One; we are only talking up a phantom.

Today's Bible texts are interpreted by three classes of minds. These three classes of minds get dealt with exactly according to their way of interpreting. The first class think that all poverty and suffering is an evidence of the punishing hand of the Almighty or his favorite's lashings. The second class think each word is to be interpreted on the mind plane, showing how our Moses thoughts act, how our Joshua thoughts act, how our mistakes get struck down when our neighbors are burned, or cycloned, or earthquaked out of existence. The third class see that there is an I AM and "I Know," the starting point within us all, which is not identified with any of our neighbors descriptions and consequences. This third class perceive that when Moses was telling the people about the goodly land awaiting them he was given his sense of what they would get by being wholly interested in the God he had set up.

Height of Mosaic Description

He told them that they would increase in cattle and gold and wines. This pleased them greatly. He warned them against forgetting to be entirely interested in his Jehovah, because he would tear them up root and branch if they should divide attentions between the goods they would soon be owning and the Jehovah who sent them. It was a hard task, he confessed, but they must do it. All of which is Mosaic description, going as far as each mind accepts. There is one I AM, and it is great "I Know." It is One. Whatever shall happen to a man who steadfastly looks back at it in himself we may get some hint of by these texts. To him shall there open up visions nearer and nearer like his native self. These visions will be to him as satisfying as gold to a Rothschild and cattle to a farmer. But, though Moses should present us with gold and wines, would they be like the visions of our own I AM and our own "I Know?"

Does the I AM store up bank notes and sheep?

So there is no temptation to look at bank notes and sheep, while the attention is satisfied with the "I Know." Yet there is no doubt whatsoever that on the journey back to our nativity we shall be dealing with all that we could ask for on each plane where we arrive.

Desideratum of the Ages

The great desideratum in all ages has been to own all things without earning them. Nothing flushes the face of a rich tradesman like being told that he came from nowhere and earned all his riches. It makes the scions of royalty look over the tops of their neighbor's heads with pride to remember that they never earned a penny, but have all their estates as gifts from the people. So Moses, catching sight of how easily our great provisions would arrive, while our actual self was being watched, told those people of cities which they never built which would be theirs and of wells, and olive trees and houses which would fall into their hands by no exertion of their own.

There is nothing like the folding tenderness of fate while our eye is on the great "I Know" just behind. There is nothing like the sheltering kindness of fate while our eye is on the great "I Know" just behind. There is nothing like the glory of life that begins and never leaves and always shields while the eye is on the great "I Know" just behind, just above, very close. Moses described it the best he could, but, truly, when the manna is falling from the great "I Know" there is no description but seems to make merchandise of its dealings as though it were give for give. But it was all ours from the beginning. We were born to it from the first, and so to have greatly cannot distract, and to know that all things are the equal possession of all men cannot engender pride.

In these verses, 3-15, Moses is telling the Hebrews the best way he can, and verily means that we cannot be distracted, and we cannot grow proud, and we cannot help spending all our breath and eyesight and life in attending the Lord our God, who is our Lord. He it is that is the one I AM equally present everywhere, first to be known as our own native, undimmable majesty, second to be seen as the "something behind." All the figurations of our neighbors which some declared were signs, while they were grinding us to the powders of shame, of our being favorites of Jehovah.

Moses spoke it the best way he knew when he said we must have nothing whatsoever to do with our neighbors' gods. In the light of the "I Know" we are able to say that truly we want nothing to do with our neighbors' gods, for the actual One is quite enough and his ways are our glory.

Chicago Inter-Ocean Newspaper, August 18, 1895

LESSON VIII

What You See Is What You Get

Joshua 3:5-17

The New York World of Sunday, August 18, has the picture of a composite "faithfully made up of twelve likenesses of the twelve most prominent new women in the world." The result, bringing out the prominent theme in each woman's mind distinctly in the composite, makes, as we might expect a terrible picture. For the twelve women are all fighters against some form of wrong and evil. They are brave fighters, implacable, tireless, stern, unyielding. This is depicted on the countenance of the "composite." The world is one great child, with invisible possibilities, like invisible hand-writings, which the heat of wise recognition will bring out. If we look at our little boy, our little girl, and suspect him or her of streaks of naughtiness, watch for those streaks, talk about those streaks, punish the little boy, punish the little girl, for what we believe them to be, we shall see those streaks increase and increase and increase till they "bring down our gray hairs with sorrow," etc., as it reads in the book of cause and consequence.

On the other hand, looking at those microcosms of possibilities we call "babies," if we suspect them of having divinity chords, immortal nobleness, we shall warm and nourish forth those streaks, and sorrow and anger will not be in us, but smiling adoration. This is truth.

"Do not look for wrong and evil;
You will find them if you do,
As you measure to your neighbor,
He will measure back to you."

What Shall be Done With the Child?

Now, with this for a fact in ethics, what shall we do with this great child namely, the congregated world? Shall we exercise the "great brains" of those women with high ideals of right and profound imaginations of wrong, in devising ways of warming forth the streaks of badness or goodness in this great child?

Where is the man, where is the woman, who can make his or her voice, or pen, or something heard on behalf of this child of infinite possibilities namely, the congregated world? There is somebody, surely there must be one motherly, wise man or woman somewhere, who is great enough, brainy enough, something enough, to command the respect of audience of thousands and thousands; such as those twelve women with the "terrible composite" are addressing, to tell the world of its majesty, its nobility, its godlikeness, and warm those hidden streaks into glorious prominence!

Up to date, those who have known about this great world baby's mighty powers have had their writings branded as "fustian" (pretentious)," typographical misrepresentations, pronounced upon as their own "ignorance," and only for the inherent potentiality of the divine facts they were proclaiming they would long since have been blotted out as very aiders and abettors of the evil streaks the "composites" of male and female "reformers" are slashing at. This because they themselves had their streaks of belief in foolishness and incompetency once warmed into prominence by private tutors and careful parents.

All in the Same Boat

The International Bible lessons always follow international experiences. We are all in the same boat as a congregated world, sailing on the sea of a never-ending eternity. We are not now viewing landscapes; we are watching each other. "Who are you?" we ask. And before they can answer we pounce upon them with our opinions of them. And our opinions always warm their own evidences into view, and we praise ourselves for being such marvelous readers of character. What saith Jesus of Nazareth, on this subject? "With what measure ye meet it shall be measured to you again." This is truth. Measuring to this great world child such brainy suspicions, what wonder the "composite" of the noted twelve maketh a terror?

Today's Bible lesson says that Joshua made a "composite" of the twelve leading men of Israel, 1451 B.C., and set them as one man to watching the absolute and eternal "I Face" of the universe.

They did not have to watch long before a mighty miracle took place. In Christian science parlance it was an "instantaneous demonstration." As the prominent women and men of our day have brought out increase of crime by seeing the face of crime and fighting crime, so these twelve prominent Israelites of antiquity brought out the face of divine majesty by facing it and adoring it. (Joshua 3:5-17)

"Yet the miracle writ on sacred page,
Can come full wrought this our age."

Moses and Joshua Compared

Moses has been taken into the beautiful kingdom of silence at the opening of this lesson and Joshua stands in his place. Joshua is more of a fighter than Moses, but whatever pounding of his enemies he does, he always does it with his eyes set toward the great "I Face" of the universe, and it does not hurt them.

He is not so great a whiner and complainer as Moses, and he does not mourn and anguish over other people's wickedness so much as Moses.

So, the original Canaanites, Hittites, Hivites, Perizzites, Girgashites, Amorites, Jebusites, who stood symbolically for those vile streaks that the brainy women are now fighting, all fled away before the composite twelve selected by Joshua, and there was left on their faces for after ages to understand, the exalted countenance, twelve in one of the Christ Jesus recognition of the divinity of man.

"Where did you hail from?" asked Jesus of man. And, when man could not yet answer by reason of having been made tongue-tied by the brainy accusers of his life, Jesus, the composite of the mother wisdom of all ages, said: *"Call no man upon the earth your father, for one is your Father, even God."*

> *"O voice over the dark waters against me!*
> *O face, through the night watching me!*
> *Hearing thee I am reassured;*
> *Seeing thee I am not afraid."*

The golden text of this lesson reads: *"When thou passeth through the waters I will be with thee."* The deepest and darkest of waters are rolling between the great world child's heavenly face and the eyes of the mothers and preachers. That deep, dark water is suspicion, and the heavenly grandeur of the congregated world is that Canaan of safety which the reformers are fighting for in a way which never had any heavenly demonstration in it yet, and never can have.

The Salvation of Scriptures

And Joshua said unto the people, *"sanctify yourselves; for tomorrow the Lord will do wonders among you."* (Verse 5) The manifestation of the divine man is what it means to "see Canaan." Making the divine man visible is what the twelve reformers of our ages are trying to do. This is called "salvation" in the sacred scriptures.

There are three salvations mentioned. That is, there are three stages of the exhibition of divine through the veils cast over the great world child's true countenance.

The first is salvation from the reformers accusing mind. This is justification. *"Believe on the Lord Jesus Christ and thou shalt be saved."* What is it to believe on the Lord? It is to recognize that he was a man insisting on his own divinity in spite of the suspicions against him, until he actually proved his own divinity. What does acknowledging this fact accomplish? It justifies all mankind in standing up and proclaiming themselves not gluttonous flesh bibbers, but sons of God.

The second exhibition of salvation is sanctification, or throwing off man's own self accusings. First, Joshua said practically, that he would acknowledge them as sons of God, but they must, secondly, help him by getting rid of their own self distrusts.

"If you distrust me, it paralyzes me at first," he said, but I can deny that you have any right to veil me over like a set of nineteenth victim of opinions. It is the same with yourselves, all of you Moses told me you were very wicked, and it has been very difficult for me to forget how you acted out his belief of you. Now, you must save yourselves from yourselves. This is sanctification. The man who can save himself from himself is sanctified, or transfigured."

Work of Twelve Just Men

All the Israelites felt the force of this eternally true proposition and to a man they tried to throw off their own self-accusings. Some tried washing in goats' blood, some went without eating, some whispered Egyptian formulas, some repeated the ten commandments, some lashed themselves, in order to whip away their own ideas of themselves, but finally Joshua had to focalize the attention of twelve men on the face of Jehovah for twenty-four hours before they could touch the third power of salvation, or the skippage of death, hell, and defeat. This last safety of man is the ultimate salvation told of in Scriptures. It is something that follows the first two-edged salvation or exhibiting of the divinity that hides in the great world child under the slurs of the savage mothers.

The last skip of man from man is miraculous. There is here nothing for man to do. The priests bare the ark and the Jordan rolled back for the children of the golden age to walk into Canaan. (Verse 17)

The section of Bible symbology tells us that the only true composite, with actual miraculous power in it, is for twelve people who do not believe in the badness of man's heart to face the great "I Face" for twenty-four hours, remembering nobody and nothing else but the immaculate mystery till the

Jordan waters of the human sorrow, poverty, defeat, and fear roll back forever from the world child's divine kingdom.

What to Expect and Believe

What a marvelous twelve shall there be, of whom these sincere women with their high ideals of good and their low estimates of the world congregation are forerunners?

There is one way for each one of us to regard himself, in spite of the cultivated streaks that our early training warmed out, and in spite of our own self-distrust. And there is one thing to expect as the golden age of prophecy now wheels its headlights into sight. Whosoever knows himself and believes in himself may expect twelve steadfast mother watchers by the flowing tide of his human life, the light of whose upturned, exalted faces, beholding not him, but the Eternal One, shall smite the mists that have veiled his life, and he shall go free — go free!

How close is the motherhood of God when the twelve single-eyed priests of antiquity and the twelve advanced women of today re-composited into one object lesson for the world child's eyes to see!

Never dawns the Christ Jesus prefigured and Joshua foreshadowed, till this world child's motherhood with one anthem pealing sings the last *Magnificat* facing Jehovah, forgetful of sin!

Chicago Inter-Ocean Newspaper, August 25, 1895

LESSON IX

Every Man To His Miracle

Joshua 6:8-20

"Beware when the great God lets loose a thinker on this planet. Then all things are at risk. It is as when conflagration has broken out in a great city, and no man knows what is safe or when it will end." — Emerson

This day's International Bible lesson strikes straight at each man's lot in life. On the plane where he walks he will have the state of affairs mentioned by these texts — Joshua 6:8-20.

If a man is walking in materiality he will find some unusual combination and work out a success for himself by it. If he is walking in mentality, or by the metaphysical knowledge which Mr. Stead, of London found so many Americans practicing, he will touch a new spring and bring out a good demonstration by it.

If a man is walking with his face set toward the unknowable and untouchable, something which forever faces him, he will seem to be doing nothing yet shall a great miracle arrive in his life.

According to the texts chosen by the International Synod this is the miracle week. Expect greatly. You cannot expect too greatly. No matter what kind of a good you have set up, he likes you to have a great confidence in him.

Alexander was proud because one of his subjects asked such a stupendous favor of him. "He remembers that I am a King!" he said, proudly. The Orientals teach their religion so as to expect great helps from their images. The Russians teach themselves to expect mighty miracles from their ikons. The Israelites hypothecated an invisible god with a temper and a generosity which always varied with their faith in him. They actually brought forth astonishing results by throwing their hearts into this invisible substance and fighting for its glory and its honor. But it is law that faith shall have its blooming demonstration in a second when we are not fighting.

"Look for the flower of the soul to bloom in the silence that follows the storm," say the mystics.

So, the lightning works. It is a long time generating, but it springs suddenly. It took a long time to undermine the Hurl-Gate (aka Hell Gate – Hudson River, NY) rocks, but a little child touched a button at the last moment and all the world heard of the miracle.

Overwhelming Power of Faith

Joshua had been urging up the faith of the Jews to white heat. The priests blew their horns with intensest confidence.

Down fell the mighty walls of Jericho while yet the Jerichoans were laughing with derision. For who could believe that a steady tone could shatter a stone wall iron bound?

It is the steadfast, unchangeable keynote that makes itself felt.

The faithful businessman must never cease expecting a great prosperity. The faithful typesetter must never cease expecting promotion of a great uplift of some sort. The faithful mother must never stop expecting great things of her boys and girls.

Expect ten-penny nails for breakfast and get them. Expect to own a farm and own one. The secret of success is the everlasting expectancy. The stopping place of expectancy with thoughts in it is when expectancy is the only thing there is of us. When we are all expectancy we do not have to think.

Jesus Christ said that the hour when we had got beyond thinking was the hour of the miracle. Joshua told the Jews that they must be profoundly silent and let the key note take care of itself. (Verse 10)

Jericho was the principal city of the land toward which the Jews journeyed. Jericho was a symbol of the principal point you have been working for. Now you are near it. Old stories are revived for our encouragement today. They were accurately told, and by reading them over and applying them to our own lives we can always tell what is coming next.

The planet vibrates as one man because of some powerful upstart of an idea held by some immovable mind.

Did not Moses tell them he was God, but they were wicked till everything he did they complained of? He measured out. "You are bad." And they measure back, "You are bad." In his heart he said: "I am God." In their hearts they said: "I am God."

Joshua said, "You are good and mighty," and they measured back to him, "You are good and mighty." Jesus said, "I am God and you are God also," and the ages are responding, "Jesus Christ is God and I am God also."

The Keynote Given by Jesus

Whatever Jesus Christ said of himself we find men now answering back of themselves. He gave a keynote and it is now reverberating from pole to pole. His keynote was: "I have come." And now the Christ Jesus in man stands up in response and says in all men everywhere: "I have come."

This wonderful something in the world child's heart can give no credit whatsoever to the social purity movers, nor to the temperance movers, nor to the pulpit preachers, nor to the school teachers, nor to the mothers and fathers: for these have all mourned over the inherent wickedness in man and have recognized that wickedness.

But Jesus Christ had a keynote on the wickedness claim and it now strikes its deathless tone through the surges of condemnation. He said: "I never knew you." Then looking straight into the ever-fronting face of Jehovah he proclaimed: "I said ye are God."

Jesus Christ was the mother of the world child. *"Call no man upon the earth your father."* How divinely beautiful is the face of a child to a mother when she sees it smile with the light of its father's eyes and lips! How divinely beautiful is the face of many to the Jesus Christ heart, for to him, man ever smiles with the glory of his Father, God.

The mother who sees the father face in her child's face typifies the Jesus Christ wisdom distinguishing the God face in all faces. Mothers often see the father sinfulness in their son's face, but to the Jesus Christ motherhood that kind of Character is never known: "I never knew you," she saith. "The heart is desperately wicked," says the Solomon style of motherhood. "I said ye are God," saith the Jesus Christ motherhood.

It is some years since the great God let loose the Jesus man on our planet but the conflagration of his kindling is begun without doubt, and where it will end is already known. The elements shall meet with fervent heat and the former ways shall be dissolved.

"The day cometh and now is" when it is better not to be out describing city slum and opium dens for describing them increases them. And the day hath come when many people know that it is better not to be studying up diseases, for they only increase by studying them up.

And so "Othello's occupation," whose keynote was badness of man, must be gone, for the Jesus Christ occupation, whose keynote is the divinity in man has begun.

Significance of the Walls of Jericho

Today's lesson declares that no matter how unreasonable it may seem to the inhabitants of Jericho that a persistent tone should break down the hard walls they will crumble nevertheless. The walls of Jericho are the hard conditions hiding the nobility and divinity and ability of every human being. The new way now set up by those who are just finding out what Jesus Christ really meant seems to be very incapable in its methods, but it is undermining everything by its keynote.

The capable things and men of materiality make a great noise. The capable things and men of divinity make no noise, make no movement. So they do not seem to be doing anything. But they are doing it all. Thus Joshua seemed to be doing nothing. The priests made all the noise. But it was the expectancy held by the silent Joshua and his silent army that broke down the walls that lay between the city and their eyes. The trumpets told nothing. They made the Jericho people laugh.

So the preaching apostles of this Jesus Christ science tell nothing. All the world says that unless these preaching apostles have got a trick worth two of the money power, the money power will soon have swallowed up the preachers as well as the factory hands.

All the world declares that unless the preachers have caught hold of some power stronger than death all the people must die within a few years. And the blaring preachers, represented by the seven priests of antiquity blowing seven rams horns, can only blare on sounding the twelve science lessons of Gabriel till the silent expectancy which fills the air of today shall suddenly crack the walls hiding a universal prosperity which shall be indeed worth two of the money power, and two of the death power, and two of every kind of power.

It was considered a great event when the twelve lessons of Gabriel science first began to blow, telling all the world that evil was all a state of mind. It was the priests going first around Jericho. It was nearer a great power when there were other blasts from the same lessons, saying that there was no evil even in mind. That was the second time around the walls of earth's troubles. It was still more powerful when the same trumpets called out that there was neither good nor evil in the absolute presence.

Summing Up the Lesson

This was the third time around humanity's hard shell of unmanageable destiny. It was a still more powerful run of the priests around human miseries when the pivotal name of the absolute one was found not to be God, nor any godly attribute or essence, but the name commanded by the writers of the four gospels. This was the fourth time around, and it seemed to be too much to expect of the trumpets that they should intensify their key. It was the fifth time around when it was found that all doctrines of men were men's own windmills whirring around, for they, at their undoctrinated center, were at their best.

It was the sixth time around when it was found that flesh life with all its joy and pain has been once lived and let go of and now no man needs to live as flesh, for something liveth for him and in him, able to do all things for him, independent of flesh. It is the seventh time around when the preaching apostles recognize that it is not their preaching that lifts the veil hiding the true face of the beautiful world child. They see that it is silent expectancy of greatness and majesty that brings them forth.

"They who talk do not know, and those who know do not talk," said wise Lao-Tzu.

All those who have preached the twelve lessons of Gabriel science have noted that the last repeat themselves over and over, making just the seventh lesson round and round. So there have never been yet given but seven lessons though they have been called twelve.

Today's Bible section tells us that the seven days' performance around Jericho was an object lesson prefiguring the end of the world by the new science, aided and abetted by world-wide expectancy. Rahab was saved on the wall of this city and was a foremother of Jesus, the wonderful, though she had a bad name.

This exhibits the glorious fact that all our doctrines of the badness of one may not hinder his or her bringing the Elohim type into view, born not of the will of flesh, but of the supernal light of recognition of Jehovah in the faces of terrible enemies.

For Rahab's eyes saw divinity where her clergymen's eyes saw enmity, and so her past was forgotten, and she only of all the cityful was capable of foremothering Jesus, in whose everlasting eyes the face of man is divine.

Chicago Inter-Ocean Newspaper, September 1, 1895

LESSON X

Every Man To His Harvest

Joshua 14:5-14

I think I could turn and live with animals;
They are so placid and self contained.
I stand and look at them long.
They do not sweat and whine about their condition;
They do not lie awake in the dark and weep for their sins;
They do not make me sick discussing their duty to God.
Not one is dissatisfied, not one is demented
With the mania of owning things;
Not one kneels to another, nor to his kind that lived thousands of years ago;
Not one is respectable or unhappy on the whole earth.
Walt Whitman

Today's International Bible lesson is a lesson in harvests. "What a man soweth that shall he also reap." This is not a miracle week for the world; it is a judgment week. The consequences of past conduct are wheeling in. The law is on hand with its meat axe of accuracy. Not a jot or tittle shall pass from the law till all be fulfilled. The Orientals have termed the harvests of life by a strange title. They call it Karma. So the world is to reap karma this week, in full precision.

The world's committee selected the texts Joshua 14:5-14, for this week because the secret principles of life pushed them to do so just as rightly as the antennae of an insect pull on the right smells and leads him to the sugar barrel.

It is the inner, invisible pressure that causes the lad to suddenly discover that he likes to invent guns better than to translate Horace. If the world had not its secret trend all set to harvesting something it has earned, the committee could have not urged us all to work ourselves up over these particular verses this week.

Caleb and Joshua had their choice of territory in the land where they had arrived, simply because they had not whined and complained. The complainers and whiners had to make their pieces of property by luck and chance, or by drawing lots. There is a mysterious push on to prosperity for the uncomplaining, cheerful man, as there is a sure field of turmoil and failure for the murmurer.

Caleb stands on the pages of illustrated religion as the everlasting cheerful, and so he got Hebron, which means alliance.

Bad Deeds Not to Be Harvested

Let the constantly cheerful person count this week on the alliance of some strong friend. Probably his best alliance would be something else. Very well. He has earned the proper alliance and it is now on hand.

One thing about this Karma crowded week is prophesied, which the religionist hardly ever permits himself to consider, and that is that the bad we have indulged in is not to be harvested.

Our good motives, our best endeavors are being weighed up and portioned out. Let none of us be envious at seeing how superior is the alliance which the cheery hearted people are getting than the weeping saints among us.

So astonished in their subconscious minds are the august selecters of texts at finding no whippings and torments laid on the children of Israel and Judah in this day's section, that some of them have devoted pages and pages to reminding us of outrageous actions of the Canaanites in the past and the equally reprehensible conduct of Joshua and his colleagues, which they all, without exception, sanctimoniously pack upon the shoulders of the God of eternity.

It is unquestioned premise that punishment for wrong actions is so much laid stress upon in religion that even the texts chosen by the synod cannot be let alone as they stand in their sublime forgetfulness of past and naughtiness. It is unquestioned premise that hardship and warfare are so much laid stress upon in religion that even the texts of this lesson cannot be let alone in their sublime indifference to fighting and bloodshed.

These texts do intimate indeed, that we are by original majesty sedate and well made and good, and therefore that all this talk about it being hard for us to act sublimely is only the insistence of the Solomon type of wisdom. He said: *"Spare the rod and spoil the child,"* but the Jesus Christ type of motherhood says: *"Of such is the kingdom of heaven."*

Today's lesson seems to point out the good streaks in humanity in a way that really acts as if the author were tired of recording crimes, and wanted to rest off a while on the records of good.

Our modern workers in the field of life never rest as is evidenced by their insisting in their comments on this Joshua week that it is silly indeed for the people of this generation to be calling for more holiness and seeking lofty spiritual attachments when they ought to be toiling, fighting, making sacrifices, and howling over their shortcomings. (Page 243: Notes on Lessons by the World Committee).

Wonderful Power of Concentration

Faithful men; they know not the principle that a man multiplies what he talks about, and decreases what he never mentions or even thinks about. The mystics tell us that by concentrating our whole mind on our own heart we shall very soon get a knowledge of the secret mental purpose of our neighbors. This lesson says that Caleb concentrated in his mind on the omnipotent Jehovah till he was as strong at eighty-five years of age as an athlete of twenty-eight.

No wonder the faces of our modern reformers all look stringy and savage if confrontation is so fruitful.

There is nothing poverty stricken about an omnipresent Jehovah, so, by concentrating on him Caleb got splendid Hebron. There is nothing wicked and sneaking about an omniscient goodness, so, by concentrating on him Caleb got a splendid character.

Blaikie, the Bible commentator, says of Caleb: "Bright and brave, strong, modest, and cheerful, there is honesty in his face, courage and decision in the very pose of his body, and the calm confidence of faith in his very look and attitude."

While the writer of this Joshua book says that this grandeur was wholly owing to his concentrated attention to an honest, holy heavenly presence in the universe and no attention whatsoever to his neighbors' actions and sufferings.

It is now being found out that the sufferings of the world are or are not, according to our concentrations. If I concentrate on the suffering of an infant or a drowning man he will be a sufferer in my estimate and groan and writhe; but if my neighbor concentrates on the free unsuffering Jehovah that is forever spreading himself through the infant and man, they will spring up free as sunshine.

All people have spells of concentrating upon prosperity and happiness. Something is always harvested from those spells of concentration. This is harvest week for our past spells of concentration on prosperity. If we had more of such spells as a world there would be more harvests like this week.

Judgment Day a Balancing Time

The judgment day is a balancing time. The sifting time, when the land promised to us we shall have in spite of the "Anakim" (giants of Hebron). Notice that Caleb says his Hebron was promised to him years and years ago. The time when Hebron was promised to him his whole heart was concentrated in confidence that this thing would be so. The "Anakim" were giants. They were determined to hold the land, but it belonged to Caleb and in the day of equity he should have it.

"The stars come nightly to the sky,
 The tidal wave unto the sea;
Nor time nor space nor deep nor high
 Can keep my own away from me."

There was a day when everybody believed, for a few moments that his life would bring forth something good. This was concentration. Those few moments have their harvest this week, in spite of the "Anakim" or living beings who seem to have all the chances. No matter at what odds those people may have on you, count on their having no power at this time.

*"This day shall shine
 To thee a star divine."*

Forevermore on Time's Wide Shore

There has been no lesson presented with so much comfort in it as this one. It has no reproach in it. It has no memory of evil in it. It has no punishment in it. It does indeed speak of the power of concentration upon some one thing, but only of concentration upon Jehovah alone. It is like Jesus speaking of the comforting love surrounding the sparrows, while the philanthropist would be seeing how many dozen birds, how many starved birds there were not knowing that there will never, never be any sinful little children to the Jesus Christ mind, and never, never any frozen sparrows to the Jesus Christ sight, for to concentrate upon Jehovah the endless and lovely is to heal the world of starvation and cold and crying and contention.

A Week of Spiritual Comfort

As this is the comforting lesson and the comforting week, it is symbol that the Holy Ghost's presence in space has been concentrated upon by somebody, and through the air globules, and through the heart granules, the smiling new mother is watching the face of a world. The motherhood of the Godhead is the Holy Ghost comforter. She is come in folds of the name of one mentioned in sacred history. She brings all things to remembrance, that were once promised unto us and we need not fret and study up the meanings of material things as related to mind, for she herself, unhelped by us, is giving them the glory that they had with us when we could hear the morning stars sing, and could see the archangels cast down their golden harps on the sweet seas of the land which we hailed from.

The metaphysician says that each one of these men stands for a trait in our mind, but who cares if they do, while the Comforter is telling of our supernal, original wisdom, which was never contaminated with symbols of mind and traits of human character?

Who cares if Caleb stands for our formulating power of mind? Who cares if Joshua stands for our saving power of mind? Who cares if Jephunneh stands for our secret antennae of mind? Who cares if we have any mind at all if the beautiful mother spirit is facing us and telling us of a transcending wisdom that is our inheritance, untouchable by ignorance, unspoilable by knowledge of good and evil?

There is something abroad in the earth which no mind can take cognizance of. A hand is on the helm of our life whose touch no words can describe.

"This is the judgment in its birth.
Tis thus our Lord approacheth earth."
Chicago Inter-Ocean Newspaper, September 8, 1895

LESSON XI

Every Man To His Refuge

Joshua 20:1-9

> *"The severe schools shall never laugh me out of the philosophy of Hermes, that this visible world is but a picture of the invisible, wherein, as in a portrait, things are not truly, but in equivocal shapes, and as they counterfeit some real substance in that invisible fabric."*
> Tomas Browne

The international lesson of September 1, told that every man might count on something out of the ordinary happening unto him during that week. Its real title was: "Every Man to His Miracle!" The lesson of September 8, told that every man might count on harvesting the fruitage of his moments of concentration on the presence of good in the universe. Its real title was, "Every Man to His Harvest!" Today's lesson tells that every man may skip the fruitage of his errors by accepting the divine scheme of erasure thereof, which divine scheme is as excellent as the erasure of mathematical mistakes on a slate.

The real title of this lesson is, "Every Man to His Refuge!" The golden text reads; *"Who have fled for refuge to lay hold upon the hope set before us."* (Hebrews 6:18)

The Bible section is chosen from Joshua 20:1-9.

"The Lord also spake unto Joshua; *"Appoint out for you cities of refuge, whereof I spake unto you by the hand of Moses."* (Verses 1 and 2)

In illustrating principles by theatricals the actors are those who are truest to facts. It is to the glory of Denman Thompson that his fellow-townsmen could not understand why there was so much fuss made over his acting exactly like characters they met every day. The rest of the religions of the globe are dismantled of their right to partiality when their lumbering illustrators are paraded before us to fix their principles in our minds. Their characters, none of them walk with such stately exactness of facts as the Jewish heroes and heroines.

So the Bible Jews have always been the best symbols of the operations of invisible principles on visible affairs. They are the most accurate theatricals we have representing religious effects. This lesson shows that no man is going to be punished for his neighbor's opinions of him. Without doubt we have all been accused of something in our lives of which we were not guilty, and without doubt we have all been accidentally involved in situations with which we had purposed to have nothing to do. This lesson declares that no man shall be hurt or disgraced or branded for any sort or kind of accidents either here or hereafter.

Comfort And Invisible City Of Refuge

In the first place every man must have his mind made up to this fact, and this will be his invisible city of refuge; and then there will certainly come into his way, or he will get into its way, some comforting event; and this will be his visible refuge. In Paul's address to the Hebrews, he speaks entirely of a mental refuge. He expects never any comfortable outward event. The Pauline golden text quoted above concerns the mental state. Paul is heavily responsible for the religious world's leaving out visible comforts in describing religious ideas. So certain have pious men been in all ages that acknowledge a divine being would plunge them into afflictions on the outward plane, but into ecstasies on the mental planes, that they have talked and talked of misery till there has seemed to be a great divorce between mind and flesh. Paul declared that his mind and body were in a continual quarrel.

These verses of Joshua, 1-17, are intended to stop the divorce business. First, mind and body must be one in eternal security, and then other kinds of divorce will cease.

This lesson hints (in verse 6) at the beautiful significance of envy, jealousy, revenge, etc., but as it is not the keynote of this lesson we will only hint at it. When we envy a man we want what he has. If we are American Indians we envy him his wampum and arrow-heads. If we are American whites we envy men their greenbacks and gold dollars.

Now, what we really want is that security from evil which wampum and gold dollars symbolize. This security is the substance of the absolute and eternal Lord Jehovah. We are doing well to be envious of the Lord Jehovah. Let man alone and envy the Lord Jehovah till we have eaten our fill of him.

For envy is an eating principle. Whoever is the subject of our envy is being subtly eaten by us, and all his doctors are wondering why he is so easily exhausted, "Who shall stand before envy?" cried Solomon. It is a greatly filling activity to envy Jehovah-jireh (the Lord will Provide), Jehovah-nissi (Jehovah is my high standard), and Jehovah-tsidkenu (the Lord our righteousness); the substance, the security, and inspiration of this universe.

What Our Sins Stand For

So with the other sins. They all stand for our throwing our arms and tongues wildly around on poor, pitiful, trembling flesh bodies, to fight and strike for what the omnipresent Jehovah really has. Thus it is an excellent sign to feel ugly and like fighting somebody, for here forever is a foeman worthy of our steel who will bear any amount of pounding and satisfy us with any amount of security.

The multitude of varieties of securities for man are called cities of refuge in this lesson. The Lord is the law of cause and effect. "The Lord spake to Joshua" the savior. The safety principle is acted out by Joshua. The delay principle, with a few miracles thrown in on an explainable basis, is acted out by Moses.

Moses psychologized the religious man with delay. Forty years of tramping through the desert marches of human hardship is the allotted drag of religious life. And of the three sacrifices we must offer up on this drag, the psychology of delay is the one religious man hugs to his bosom hardest.

Our poetry reads that the mills of the gods grind slowly. Our preachers strike the air with the palms of their hands and declare that "forty is consecrated to affliction by the spirit of love." But this is nothing but hypnotism. The refuge from the triple-plated psychology of the law of cause and consequence wrapped around man is in sacrifice of three teachings. Sacrifice is laid great stress upon in the Bible because sacrifice is so enchantingly unburdening. Sacrifice the psychology that you have to get your freedom by stages and steps. That freedom is now just as it always was. Sacrifice, the psychology that it takes time to find your vantage ground. That vantage ground is now just as it always was, under your own feet. Sacrifice, the psychology that something in the universe interferes with you. The theory of interference is the third "lamina" (layer). With these coats on, you cannot flee to your refuge so swiftly as to find that you are already free, wise, immortal substance, now, and have been so since,

Before ever the atoms did come and go
In the surging tide of the soundless sea,
Whose billows from nowhere to nowhere flow
As they break on the sands of eternity."

The Philosophy of Hermes

A theory is a mental postulate. It is beginning to be honestly believed that mental postulates formulate into outward affairs. This is the philosophy of Hermes, to which Sir Thomas Browne, referred. Joel prophesied that in the closing up days of the psychologized state of mankind, men would climb up walls and enter into buildings without making any sounds at all. That means that they shall run around with their thoughts. He says they shall fall on their own swords and not hurt themselves. That means that their own mistakes cannot hurt them whether they were accidents of mind or body, for they shall drop into the security that has lain under their feet since before eternity had a name.

On whatever plane we wander there is a state of security there for us. If we have on no heavy coats of the psychology of time, danger and interference, we are secure everywhere. So the playwrights depicting how far mental securities could be counted on and how far bodily securities could be counted on, called the safe status of mind and body "cities of refuge," and all the time they instructed their listeners and readers that these "cities of refuge" symbolized an absolute state of safety, not only from neighbors' opinions of us, but from accidents of time and space and mind.

The cities mentioned in verses 7 and 8 signify the different states of mind which are safe for us when we are full of different kinds of blundering. Any Bible dictionary will give the meaning of "Kedish in Galilee," "Shechem in Mount Ephraim," "Bezer of Reuben," "Ramath in Gilead," etc., and those who are interested in ferreting out thoughts and their results may spend whole sermons ramifying around into the relations between thoughts and things, but these Bible lessons do not point that way, they point to the Christian scheme of absolute refuge, unburdened of coats of psychology by the acceptance of the un-psychologized fact always under our feet, which is even nearer at hand than the symbolic near cities of ancient Israel.

Paul Found Refuge In Christ

Paul said he had fled for refuge to Christ Jesus, who was the one man of all the countless millions on this globe who had fled into the city of safety under foot everywhere, by dissolving the copper-plate of time, and the steel coat of distance, and the wire netting of interference, till his free substance had stood forth identical with original God.

Paul felt confident that none of us could work out of the psychologic plates of time, terror, and interference so quickly as by accepting the fact that, as by the Mosaic plan, man would be perpetually shuffling off conditions and dodging consequences, which are the curse; by the mysteriously stupendous achievement of Jesus there is no curse felt except where we choose to lug one, *"Christ hath redeemed us from the curse of the law, being made a curse for us."* (Gal, 3:18)

As this Jesus tore off the psychologic coats for himself and showed himself free, untrammeled existence forever, saying as he dropped even the weight of the eye of man on his ascending splendor; "Thus it behooved Christ to suffer and to rise." It is the fulfillment of the prophetic theatricals of Joshua for every man now to flee from the consequences of his errors to some refuge.

And it most certainly is the whole scheme of Old Testament illustration to point to some quick touch of foot and mind on the secure place under our feet. The New Testament dispensation declares that one man's refuge is all men's refuge the instant he makes it, because men are so linked shoulder to shoulder in contagious existence. "In thy light I see light." "In thy freedom I go free," "In thy refuge I am safe." "In thy uplifting up I am lifted up," "In thy un-psychologized originality I am uncoated nativity."

Chicago Inter-Ocean Newspaper September 15, 1895

LESSON XII

The Twelve Propositions

Joshua 24:14-25

This lesson of today teaches about the human mind and how to rescue it from the clutches of the two opposing movements of good and evil.

It does not enter into the details of deep metaphysics at all. If it did, it would explain how there is no human mind left after its rescue from good and evil. Dante struck more deeply into the science of mind when he said "God is above goodness and virtue," for me by this affirmation, takes mind out of its habitat and uncoats it of its last idea. We all realize that mind insists, as long as it can move, upon something good or evil.

Primitive Christian science taught all about the power and substantiality of the good. It denied the power and the substance of evil. For every one of its twelve propositions there is a confirmation in the Bible, in the Bhagavad Gita, and in the Book of the Dead.

The Christian science now showing its unspeakably beautiful face in the parting crevice made by the doctrine swing of evil off to the left and of the good off to the right, is unidentified with either good and evil. It deals with the uncontaminated One. For the mysterious science there are confirmations in the Bible, the books of the Zend, the Vedas, the Laws of Manu, and even in the Book of the Dead.

But this Joshua lesson is distinctly and definitely dealing with primitive Christian science and its plainly divided twelve points:

1. Statement of omnipresence.
2. Denial of two presences.
3. Affirmation of omnipresence.
4. Faith.
5. Works.
6. Understanding.
7. Denial of flesh birth.
8. Denial of appearances.
9. Denial of sin.
10. Affirmation of equal divinity in all men.
11. Affirmation of equal intelligence in all.
12. Affirmation of equal spiritual ability in all.

These were first explained at length as Mosaic order in twelve printed Lessons in Christian Science, and have since been simplified in a beautiful fashion by H.M. Stowe, J.W. Yarnall, E.J. Castle, H. Van Anderson and others.

For each statement in order there was certain to be an outward demonstration corresponding in splendor and definitions with the plane upon which the thinker was living and for each one of the statements in order there was a statement by Jesus of Nazareth:

1. God is spirit, and they who worship must worship in spirit.
2. Ye are of your father, the devil, liar from the beginning.
3. The Father and I are one. I in you.
4. Ye believe in God — believe also in me.
5. These signs shall follow them that believe.
6. I will give you a mouth, and wisdom which no man shall be able to gainsay, nor resist. God giveth not the Spirit by measure.
7. Call no man upon earth your father.
8. Ye are the light. Judge not according to appearances.
9. I came not to condemn the world.
10. One is your Father. My word shall not pass away.
11. Ye all know whence I came. The Holy Ghost shall teach you all things.
12. All that I have heard from the Father I have told you. Your joy no man taketh from you.

Strange Similarity in Teaching

For each of these statements in order there is one almost identical in every old religious book on earth. Even in that work on magic, Ennemoser, translated and commented on by William and Mary Howitt, in 1854, there is a statement corresponding so closely with the Christian science proclamation enunciated by P.P. Quimby and M.B.G. Eddy that these writers might also be accredited with having studied Ennemoser's "History of Magic." In that book all phantoms of evil are explained as delusions of mind; the one universal healing presence is wonderfully described, the divinity of man is announced, and miracles are shown to be his natural abilities exposing themselves.

The theosophists have translated from the Sanscrit a work on rajah yoga, in which these twelve lessons have their identical correspondence:

1. Bram is the all pervading One.
2. The world is all atma, and nothing else but atma.
3. Sitting in a solitary place, being desireless, curbing passions, one should meditate upon the identification of one's self with that atma who is one and has no distinction of place, time, and things. I am that very Brahm.
4. As the identity and unification of oneself and atma is known, the belief that himself

in body, senses, etc., will vanish, and one will see in one-self that undivided and indivisible atma.

5. The meaning of Brahma is the Ever Great. A man becomes that on which he persistently thinks.

6. All this universe, visible or invisible, the seer, the seen, the sight is one consciousness. The enlightened will through his mind be ever filled with the bliss of identifying himself with universal consciousness.

7. He who is free from the great bondage of desire, so difficult to avoid is alone capable of liberation; not another even though versed in the six systems of philosophy.

8. Disease is never cured by pronouncing the name of a medicine without taking it, so liberation is not achieved by the pronunciation of the word Brahm without direct perception. Pure consciousness is in all supreme spirit.

9. Deprived of the real knowledge of the atma through being devoured by the spark of great delusion, the man becomes contemptible in conduct. The properties of pure satva are purity, perception of the atma within us, cheerfulness, concentration of mind on the self, by which a state of eternal bliss is obtained.

10. <u>A wise man must acquire the discrimination of spirit and not-spirit in all things.</u>
11. <u>Ignorance has no beginning, and this also applies to its effects. The knowledge that Brahm and atma are one and the same, is true knowledge. This can only be acquired by the perfect discrimination of ego and non-ego. Ego is the "I" that ordains and knows. The non-ego seems to ordain and know but is nothing.</u>
12. <u>By the absence of all existence besides itself this Brahm is supreme.</u>

<u>Law of the Covenant Imperative</u>

Joshua has a way of ignoring the evil of human life, which is equivalent to denying it, but when he speaks of a man's getting into the consequences of wrong beliefs he shows how inexcitable and merciless the law of cause and effect is. He calls the law of cause and consequence "Lord." He never calls it God over man when man lives with his neck under its yoke. He tells the quaking of Jews that this Lord is a jealous God, and will not forgive their transgressions nor their sins. (Verse 19) He then proceeds to tell them the twelve covenants, which every man must make between his mighty God and himself.

The law of the covenant is imperative. All religion is covenanting. If I say that there is one mighty presence filling heaven and earth, I am covenanting with that presence to believe in it. Then I shall become more aware of this presence by telling about it. I am in the teeth of the consequences of my belief. As it is very good and strengthening to believe in a mighty one filling my body and mind and the stars and the acorn seeds, I shall be pleased with what happens to me as a consequence of that covenant.

But now suppose I tell of this mighty one and then tell some wicked principle going around making some people thieves, some opium eaters, some liars, some cowards, etc.? Then I am covenanting with two governors, and both these governors have their ways of coming down on me at the proper moment with their different kinds of effects. It is not strengthening to covenant with a hateful governor, like that one who makes cowards and sneaks, so I shall be very miserable. Then I shall lay it all to the Mighty One filling all space. I shall say that it is very strange indeed that such a good presence is so hateful to me making me sick half the time and deaf all the time. Then I shall about that time find the good governor's time is up for rewarding that talk I once used praising him up for his mighty powers of life and health and prosperity. Then I shall say that my afflictions were strung on my neck by this same "him," and so I shall go up and down, up and down, varying my experiences with darks and lights, because I have two governors with whom I have covenanted unknowingly.

Joshua said: "And if it seem evil unto you to serve the Lord, choose ye this day who ye will serve; whether the gods which your fathers served, that were on the other side of the flood, or the gods of the Amorites, in whose land ye dwell; but as for me and my house, we will serve the Lord."

Choice Given the Israelites

By this he means that he shall not believe matter as having any power over him. It is Egyptian darkness when a man thinks small pox, or blind eyes, or amputated limbs have any power or ways of their own which they are bound to carry out. It is Amorite darkness when a man thinks other men are stronger than he is, or weaker than he is on the account of personal defects or personal advantages. It is not claimed by anybody that Joshua knew that material substances have no reality, but he unconsciously talked that way, giving all power to the universal spirit always and this made him strong and intelligent.

The people had said so much about the evils which the Lord had visited on them, that he had to ask them to decide whether the Lord was such a terrible visitor that they would rather have nothing to do with him or if they should stand up and covenant that the mighty presence filling the earth should have his own way with them. It was because Joshua was so persistent in giving all power and great kindliness to the Universal One that the Israelites finally got out of the deserts. It is very plain that Joshua thought all their afflictions were punishments for something, but he most certainly never knew that it was because they talked of evil and watched for evil and dreaded evil and prayed over evil so much that they covenanted with the laws more than with the good.

It seems to have been Joshua's cheerful optimism, giving the great Jehovah all the glory for every good event, and saying so very little about evil events, that made him so mighty in character.

It is true now, as then, that watching this mighty presence, putting up the hands toward it, walking the feet over it, moving the body through it, speaking often unto it, will make a weak person strong, will beautify a homely person, will heal a sick person, make wise a foolish person, and make an unfortunate person prosperous.

It had not been good for the Jews to attribute so much affliction and punishment to a presence they had covenanted with to believe in as merciful, loving, generous, and they had been pulled and twisted for many years between the two natures they had described, but Joshua had kept very silent on the evils of life, so his affirmations of good had got them safety through the deserts. (Verse 17)

Question of Evil Must Be Settled

Jesus taught not only the policy of silence on the subject of evil and the self-directions of matter, but he taught positive denial of them. "If any man will come after me, let him deny himself." "Sit thou on the right hand." The reason the Orientals have not shown any living beauty, any mighty kindness to their hordes and swarms of starving children is because they did not take as positive denials of evil as they did of matter. They can dissolve stones and glassware by dematerializing words, but they have instructed their little victim The Dalai Lama to repeat over and over, age in age out, whenever they bring him forth that this is a sorrowful, sorrowful, miserable, miserable world.

The question of evil has to be settled before the question of matter is manageable. A man's stealing must be as near nothing as his bones, in our wisdom lighted eyes, if we want to see his majesty.

Evil was dissolvable as matter to him that knows it is the product of his own word and his word is his Lord forever.

Jesus did, indeed, teach that there should come a time when Joshua's tacit denial by not speaking of evil should be put into positive statements and that after man had seen that his good was as much the product of his talking and writing as evil had ever been, and that good was no more the actual nature of this wonderful presence than evil is its nature, that then a new heaven and a new earth should smile through the parting curtains of the pairs of departing opposites. He promised the sight of an undescribable dwelling place. He promised an unthinkable revelation.

While I say there is evil in anybody or in any place, I am not watching the good and finding its omnipresent face. While I say the good is everywhere and I see no evil, I have not even the unspeakable wonder called in our Bible the new heaven and the new earth. And so this Joshua lesson talks of the all good it leaves us just here.

Chicago Inter-Ocean Newspaper, September 22, 1895

LESSON XIII

Review

I Kings 8:56

*Who shall say that the crocus so prompt
Is a bit premature under gray sky's haunt?
How about the thistle, with her pink spring crown-
Does she not know her business, though husband-
men frown?
And the regal chrysanthemum, enchanting with
cheer
At the season of frost - do you think she is queer
To risk the vantage ground an old year?*
                                            Wetmore

The golden text of today's International Bible lesson means the same as the above verse, namely, that nobody and nothing can possibly fail to bloom out in all the glory of that unto which they were appointed.

The golden text reads: *"There hath not failed one word of all his good promise, which he prom-*

ised by the hand of Moses his servant." (I Kings 8:56)

Of course, Moses represents the law of cause and effect as it works on every plane. This law is the servant of the originator of law. Jesus of Nazareth struck the authoritative attitude where nothing could carry out its destiny to save its life. He struck the flourishing fig tree with a word and it ceased its flourishing. He touched the vigorous swine with a movement of his commanding energy and they disappeared at once. Their prime of bloom they seemed to fail to know. Is there any discrepancy between the ideas that everything reaches its appointed glory and yet that nothing is safe if a Jesus is near?

There is none. The flowers and the swine are but emblems. The emblem never is anything but a picture of the substance behind it. The picture is erasable, but the substance behind it is indestructible.

It is the province of the inner interpretations of the Bible to turn our attention to the substance behind the emblem, till we are so substantial that we can make as many pictures as we please. We can put any kind of a picture any where we please. We can put a well and beautiful body where there was a sick one, or like Peter we can brush it out of sight altogether. The emblem is changeable, but the substance is unchangeable.

Reference of the Golden Text

The golden text refers to a wonderful fact concerning the man who touches the substance behind the pictures. He never wants to blot out anything beautiful or kind or glorifying. He loves the present order of summer and winter; seed time and harvest; he loves to see the worm run in undisturbed glee and the elephant move in fearless majesty. He falls in with the present order in every respect except that he erases pain, discord, cruelty, greed, crime.

It is the nature of the man whose eye is on the substance back of the rose to let the rose bloom undisturbed by worms or fading. It is the nature of the man with his eye on the true substance to show how the same rose that blooms is but dipping itself backward into its original substance when we are seeing it die, and if we see the substance we can see the rose at its bath in substance with which it renews itself for fresh budding.

It is the nature of a man with his eye on the changeless substance to satisfy everything and everybody with twelve kinds of beauty. He is to all things a tree of life bringing forth twelve manner of fruits. There is no hurt in his ministry. There is no power to hurt given to anything or permitted to anything in the presence of a man whose eye is on the fadeless something behind everything.

This is not new doctrine. Every religion and every historic reasoning has the same assurance. Keep you eye on the eternal and your intellect will grow, said Emerson. Then Jesus said there will be no end to its increasement. With his eye on the everlasting one, all man's presence is life to his neighbor, say the old reasoners.

If this is not true, then there is nothing worth investigating, for there's only a round and round of pleasure and pain forever. It is because there are transcendental lessons given forth age after age that the chrysanthemum comes expectantly on the old year's chill and wins as much praise as the crocus of spring. It is because of transcendental lessons from age to age that the promises of the prophets come true, saying that prosperity, and greatness should come, despite oppositions.

Pain not in the Gift of the Eternal

They sided with the something behind everything and its nature is to beautify and happify. There is no death in its droppings. There is no pain in its droppings. If a man says pain is in the gift of the Eternal, he shows that he is not seeing the Eternal; if a man says that afflictions are the gift of the Eternal, he shows that he is not watching the eternal something behind everything.

With each one's eye on the eternal each one would see himself in his bloom of power and success, and nothing could make him see defeat. He would see that, like the chrysanthemum sturdily glorifying in frost, he was most mighty when hope and faith were at lowest ebb.

There is much talk about faith in what is not visible as bringing it into visibility, but Esther had no faith when she faced the terrible Xerxes, and great Mordecai had no faith in her, yet with her eye on the Eternal her life and the life of her people flourished.

It does not read that our eye is to be held on the intellect, imagining it strong for a suitable length of time, but it says: "Eye on the Eternal." It is not "eye on the healthy body," but "eye on the something behind the body." *"Look unto me and be ye saved."* It is because somebody's eye is always somewhat and somewhere on the Eternal that so much good and life reign in this world. It is not faith in it that pulls its strings of strength, but watching it, faith or no faith.

Moses watched the Eternal enough so that mighty miracles rained down for the sake of the Jews. Joshua watched it so that mighty miracles rained down on them. Jesus watched it so steadily that miracles are still raining down on a world and still more mighty miracles are at our gates.

Man was breathing atmospheric air in a vigorous manner till on a day he set his gaze on the Eternal in the air and that made him a living soul. To this day a breath of a man is nothing but picture till he recognizes in it the divine elixirs and then he touches substance through it so that his life bounds with new energy. Primitive religion taught mankind to look forward into space as though looking at a fine point and to breathe into the nostrils deep down into the system, the word Om.

No Past, No Future, No Present

This was hint but no explanation of the finer direction to watch the Eternal. The people who practiced it were seeking wisdom. They wanted power over the grave and bodily sensations. You can judge for yourself whether what they secured by practicing deaths and gazings and whisperings is of great value. To this eternal there is no present to it. Though every good and perfect gift droppeth down from the substance it is by itself tireless, fadeless, moveless.

This lesson is a review. It takes up the miracles that fell on the Jews because of somebody's watch on the Eternal, or it takes up the watch over again with renewed attentiveness. If we are greatly concerned over worms and elephants, over Joshua's slaughters and the temper of Moses, we shall have the name of being great memorizers and so our review will please people who live in pictures. If we are wholly occupied with gazing on the mighty substance back of the pictures we shall have the name of knowing nothing, yet our very presence in the room shall save from sickness and death.

It is not possible that remembering the names of the bones in the ear will cure deafness, but it is possible that by remembering the substances back of the bones deafness will flee away.

The ears shall dip back into their original substance for him that reviews their nameless original, and they shall live as restless pictures on the canvas of time. When Jesus blasted the fig tree and erased the swine, he was exhibiting the originating substance as capable of undoing and redoing its own pictures. But over and over he told of his word as life and restoration and not destructiveness. He restored the tree when he pleased and returned the unkillable beasts to their native pastures when he saw fit.

No Promise Given Shall Fail

The times and seasons of things were in this appointment, and their beauty was as fresh; when newly come from their last bath after eons of reblooming from that which was behind them, as when just they sprang up from its bosom.

Not one word of the promises of each man shall fail him. His greatness shall stand out in its bloom as a picture of splendor on the spring grass like a crocus, or on the November snows like a frost flower. The golden text is chosen to teach a man to have faith that what has been promised shall come, but its deepest significance is that whoever looks into the face of that which is near by forever, from which he came forth, shall realize his bloom of greatness and power and his season of majesty shall never drop its head into decrepitude and misfortune. In all spiritual science great stress is laid upon realization of the divine presence. It is said that realization of this presence is always followed by miracles. So the spiritually minded are always searching around after realizations of the divine presence. But realization is not first. It is second. Watch the great one and realization is sure.

Man in the Beginning, Beautiful

Every watcher of the mighty one sees himself at his beginning and never sees himself any other way. How was he at his beginning, before the earth wheeled off from the sun and before the sun ran away from its mother globe in its old home far beyond the faintest stars' picture on the lens of the greatest telescope?

He was so wonderful in beauty, power, goodness, and majesty that even the awful God pronounced him "very good."

To the world-taught eye he is a fading and sinful creature, worm-eaten and full of ungodly ways.

He seems to be delayed in showing his powers and seems to need much study to make him know how even to make his bread; but to himself his fadeless and unfailing bloom is always as fair at first, and when he sees the Eternal, and in seeing it sees himself, his neighbors follow his lead and see as he sees.

The Last Enemy to Be Overthrown

There is no other review worth counting save the review of the Eternal Something Behind. There is no other fact worth touching save that substance into which the flowers dip when we say they die, and into which our people plunge when we say they die, for there is where they all see that their path in it is their turning around to return here again and again. And there is where they see, that they need not see, to die and spoil while they are turning around into their original substance, but may show every moment a new beauty and power which can round the circle into bud and bloom again without spoiling.

This is the final miracle of watching the Eternal. "The last enemy to be over thrown is death." With such a miracle morning in Paradise dawns. Watching the Eternal, Jesus knew himself and realized his own mightiness. Though a man were a hod carrier, yet should he see himself as mighty as Jesus by watching the same one whom Jesus watched, and though he were a duke he could see no more.

The deeper sense of the golden text and the sweet verses would be that everything has its bloom which only he who sees the substance back of the bloom can keep everlasting trace of, and that the promise of changeless brightness is an unfailing promise.

Chicago Inter-Ocean Newspaper, September 29, 1895

Notes

Other Books by Emma Curtis Hopkins

- *Class Lessons of 1888 (WiseWoman Press)*
- *Bible Interpretations (WiseWoman Press)*
- *Esoteric Philosophy in Spiritual Science (WiseWoman Press)*
- *Genesis Series 1894 (WiseWoman Press)*
- *High Mysticism (WiseWoman Press)*
- *Self Treatments with Radiant I Am (WiseWoman Press)*
- *Gospel Series (WiseWoman Press)*
- *Judgment Series in Spiritual Science (WiseWoman Press)*
- *Drops of Gold (WiseWoman Press)*
- *Resume (WiseWoman Press)*
- *Scientific Christian Mental Practice (DeVorss)*

Books about Emma Curtis Hopkins and her teachings

- *Emma Curtis Hopkins, Forgotten Founder of New Thought* – Gail Harley
- *Unveiling Your Hidden Power: Emma Curtis Hopkins' Metaphysics for the 21st Century (also as a Workbook and as A Guide for Teachers)* – Ruth L. Miller
- *Power to Heal: Easy reading biography for all ages* –Ruth Miller

To find more of Emma's work, including some previously unpublished material, log on to:

www.highwatch.org

www.emmacurtishopkins.com

WISEWOMAN PRESS

Vancouver, WA 98665
800.603.3005
www.wisewomanpress.com

Books Published by WiseWoman Press

By Emma Curtis Hopkins

- *Resume*
- *Gospel Series*
- *Class Lessons of 1888*
- *Self Treatments including Radiant I Am*
- *High Mysticism*
- *Genesis Series 1894*
- *Esoteric Philosophy in Spiritual Science*
- *Drops of Gold Journal*
- *Judgment Series*
- *Bible Interpretations: Series I, thru XVII*

By Ruth L. Miller

- *Unveiling Your Hidden Power: Emma Curtis Hopkins' Metaphysics for the 21st Century*
- *Coming into Freedom: Emily Cady's Lessons in Truth for the 21st Century*
- *150 Years of Healing: The Founders and Science of New Thought*
- *Power Beyond Magic: Ernest Holmes Biography*
- *Power to Heal: Emma Curtis Hopkins Biography*
- *The Power of Unity: Charles Fillmore Biography*
- *Power of Thought: Phineas P. Quimby Biography*
- *The Power of Insight: Thomas Troward Biography*
- *The Power of Mind: Ralph Waldo Emerson Biography*
- *Gracie's Adventures with God*
- *Uncommon Prayer*
- *Spiritual Success*
- *Finding the Path*

www.wisewomanpress.com

List of Bible Interpretation Series, with dates, First to Twenty-second Series

This list is for the First to the Twewnty-second Series. Emma produced twenty-eight Series of Bible Interpretations.

She followed the Bible Passages provided by the International Committee of Clerics who produced the Bible Quotations for each year's use in churches all over the world.

Emma used these for her column of Bible Interpretations in both the Christian Science Magazine, at her Seminary and in the Chicago Inter-Ocean Newspaper.

First Series

July 5 - September 27, 1891

Lesson 1	The Word Made Flesh	July 5th
	John 1:1-18	
Lesson 2	Christ's First Disciples	July 12th
	John 1:29-42	
Lesson 3	All Is Divine Order	July 19th
	*John 2:1-1*1 (Christ's first Miracle)	
Lesson 4	Jesus Christ and Nicodemus	July 26th
	John 3:1-17	
Lesson 5	Christ at Samaria	August 2nd
	John 4:5-26 (Christ at Jacob's Well)	
Lesson 6	Self-condemnation	August 9th
	John 5:17-30 (Christ's Authority)	
Lesson 7	Feeding the Starving	August 16th
	John 6:1-14 (The Five Thousand Fed)	
Lesson 8	The Bread of Life	August 23rd
	John 6:26-40 (Christ the Bread of Life)	
Lesson 9	The Chief Thought	August 30th
	John 7:31-34 (Christ at the Feast)	
Lesson 10	Continue the Work	September 6th
	John 8:31-47	
Lesson 11	Inheritance of Sin	September 13th
	John 9:1-11, 35-38 (Christ and the Blind Man)	
Lesson 12	The Real Kingdom	September 20th
	John 10:1-16 (Christ the Good Shepherd)	
Lesson 13	In Retrospection	September 27th
	Review	

Second Series

October 4 - December 27, 1891

Lesson 1	Mary and Martha *John 11:21-44*	October 4th
Lesson 2	Glory of Christ *John 12:20-36*	October 11th
Lesson 3	Good in Sacrifice *John 13:1-17*	October 18th
Lesson 4	Power of the Mind *John 14:13; 15-27*	October 25th
Lesson 5	Vines and Branches *John 15:1-16*	November 1st
Lesson 6	Your Idea of God *John 16:1-15*	November 8th
Lesson 7	Magic of His Name *John 17:1-19*	November 15th
Lesson 8	Jesus and Judas *John 18:1-13*	November 22nd
Lesson 9	Scourge of Tongues *John 19:1-16*	November 29th
Lesson 10	Simplicity of Faith *John 19:17-30*	December 6th
Lesson 11	Christ is All in All *John 20: 1-18*	December 13th
Lesson 12	Risen With Christ *John 21:1-14*	December 20th
Lesson 13	The Spirit is Able Review of Year	December 27th

Third Series

January 3 - March 27, 1892

Lesson 1	A Golden Promise *Isaiah 11:1-10*	January 3rd
Lesson 2	The Twelve Gates *Isaiah 26:1-10*	January 10th
Lesson 3	Who Are Drunkards *Isaiah 28:1-13*	January 17th
Lesson 4	Awake Thou That Sleepest *Isaiah 37:1-21*	January 24th
Lesson 5	The Healing Light *Isaiah 53:1-21*	January 31st
Lesson 6	True Ideal of God *Isaiah 55:1-13*	February 7th
Lesson 7	Heaven Around Us *Jeremiah 31 14-37*	February 14th
Lesson 8	But One Substance *Jeremiah 36:19-31*	February 21st
Lesson 9	Justice of Jehovah *Jeremiah 37:11-21*	February 28th
Lesson 10	God and Man Are One *Jeremiah 39:1-10*	March 6th
Lesson 11	Spiritual Ideas *Ezekiel 4:9, 36:25-38*	March 13th
Lesson 12	All Flesh is Grass *Isaiah 40:1-10*	March 20th
Lesson 13	The Old and New Contrasted Review	March 27th

Fourth Series

April 3 - June 26, 1892

Lesson 1	Realm of Thought *Psalm 1:1-6*	April 3rd
Lesson 2	The Power of Faith *Psalm 2:1-12*	April 10th
Lesson 3	Let the Spirit Work *Psalm 19:1-14*	April 17th
Lesson 4	Christ is Dominion *Psalm 23:1-6*	April 24th
Lesson 5	External or Mystic *Psalm 51:1-13*	May 1st
Lesson 6	Value of Early Beliefs *Psalm 72:1-9*	May 8th
Lesson 7	Truth Makes Free *Psalm 84:1-12*	May 15th
Lesson 8	False Ideas of God *Psalm 103:1-22*	May 22nd
Lesson 9	But Men Must Work *Daniel 1:8-21*	May 29th
Lesson 10	Artificial Helps *Daniel 2:36-49*	June 5th
Lesson 11	Dwelling in Perfect Life *Daniel 3:18-25*	June 12th
Lesson 12	Which Streak Shall Rule *Daniel 6:16-28*	June 19th
Lesson 13	See Things as They Are Review of 12 Lessons	June 26th

Fifth Series

July 3 - September 18, 1892

Lesson 1	The Measure of a Master *Acts 1:1-12*	July 3rd
Lesson 2	Chief Ideas Rule People *Acts 2:1-12*	July 10th
Lesson 3	New Ideas About Healing *Acts 2:37-47*	July 17th
Lesson 4	Heaven a State of Mind *Acts 3:1-16*	July 24th
Lesson 5	About Mesmeric Powers *Acts 4:1-18*	July 31st
Lesson 6	Points in the Mosaic Law *Acts 4:19-31*	August 7th
Lesson 7	Napoleon's Ambition *Acts 5:1-11*	August 14th
Lesson 8	A River Within the Heart *Acts 5:25-41*	August 21st
Lesson 9	The Answering of Prayer *Acts 7: 54-60 - Acts 8: 1-4*	August 28th
Lesson 10	Words Spoken by the Mind *Acts 8:5-35*	September 4th
Lesson 11	Just What It Teaches Us *Acts 8:26-40*	September 11th
Lesson 12	The Healing Principle Review	September 18th

Sixth Series

September 25 - December 18, 1892

Lesson 1	The Science of Christ *1 Corinthians 11:23-34*	September 25th
Lesson 2	On the Healing of Saul *Acts 9:1-31*	October 2nd
Lesson 3	The Power of the Mind Explained *Acts 9:32-43*	October 9th
Lesson 4	Faith in Good to Come *Acts 10:1-20*	October 16th
Lesson 5	Emerson's Great Task *Acts 10:30-48*	October 23rd
Lesson 6	The Teaching of Freedom *Acts 11:19-30*	October 30th
Lesson 7	Seek and Ye Shall Find *Acts 12:1-17*	November 6th
Lesson 8	The Ministry of the Holy Mother *Acts 13:1-13*	November 13th
Lesson 9	The Power of Lofty Ideas *Acts 13:26-43*	November 20th
Lesson 10	Sure Recipe for Old Age *Acts 13:44-52, 14:1-7*	November 27th
Lesson 11	The Healing Principle *Acts 14:8-22*	December 4th
Lesson 12	Washington's Vision *Acts 15:12-29*	December 11th
Lesson 13	Review of the Quarter	December 18th
	Partial Lesson Shepherds and the Star	December 25th

Seventh Series

January 1 - March 31, 1893

Lesson 1	All is as Allah Wills *Ezra 1*	January 1st
Lesson 2	Zerubbabel's High Ideal *Ezra 2:8-13*	January 8th
Lesson 3	Divine Rays Of Power *Ezra 4*	January 15th
Lesson 4	Visions Of Zechariah *Zechariah 3*	January 22nd
Lesson 5	Spirit of the Land *Zechariah 4:1-10*	January 27th
Lesson 6	Dedicating the Temple *Ezra 6:14-22*	February 3rd
Lesson 7	Nehemiah's Prayer *Nehemiah 13*	February 12th
Lesson 8	Ancient Religions *Nehemiah 4*	February 19th
Lesson 9	Understanding is Strength Part 1 *Nehemiah 13*	February 26th
Lesson 10	Understanding is Strength Part 2 *Nehemiah 13*	March 3rd
Lesson 11	Way of the Spirit *Esther*	March 10th
Lesson 12	Speaking of Right Things *Proverbs 23:15-23*	March 17th
Lesson 13	Review	March 24th

Eighth Series

April 2 - June 25, 1893

Lesson 1	The Resurrection of Christ *Matthew 28:1-10*	April 2nd
Lesson 2	Universal Energy *Book of Job, Part 1*	April 9th
Lesson 3	Strength From Confidence *Book of Job, Part II*	April 16th
Lesson 4	The New Doctrine Brought Out *Book of Job, Part III*	April 23rd
Lesson 5	Wisdom's Warning *Proverbs 1:20-23*	April 30th
Lesson 6	The Law of Understanding *Proverbs 3*	May 7th
Lesson 7	Self-Esteem *Proverbs 12:1-15*	May 14th
Lesson 8	Physical vs. Spiritual Power *Proverbs 23:29-35*	May 21st
Lesson 9	Only One Power (information taken from Review)	May 28th
Lesson 10	Recognizing Our Spiritual Nature *Proverbs 31:10-31*	June 4th
Lesson 11	Intuition *Ezekiel 8:2-3, Ezekiel 9:3-6, 11*	June 11th
Lesson 12	The Power of Faith *Malachi*	June 18th
Lesson 13	Review of the 2nd Quarter *Proverbs 31:10-31*	June 25th

Ninth Series

July 2 - September 27, 1893

Lesson 1	Secret of all Power *Acts 16: 6-15*	July 2nd
Lesson 2	The Flame of Spiritual Verity *Acts 16:18*	July 9th
Lesson 3	Healing Energy Gifts *Acts 18:19-21*	July 16th
Lesson 4	Be Still My Soul *Acts 17:16-24*	July 23rd
Lesson 5	(Missing) Acts 18:1-11	July 30th
Lesson 6	Missing No Lesson *	August 6th
Lesson 7	The Comforter is the Holy Ghost *Acts 20*	August 13th
Lesson 8	Conscious of a Lofty Purpose *Acts 21*	August 20th
Lesson 9	Measure of Understanding *Acts 24:19-32*	August 27th
Lesson 10	The Angels of Paul *Acts 23:25-26*	September 3rd
Lesson 11	The Hope of Israel *Acts 28:20-31*	September 10th
Lesson 12	Joy in the Holy Ghost *Romans 14*	September 17th
Lesson 13	Review *Acts 26-19-32*	September 24th

Tenth Series

October 1 – December 24, 1893

Lesson 1	When the Truth is Known *Romans 1:1-19*	October 1st
Lesson 2	Justification, free grace, redemption *Romans 3:19-26*	October 8th.
Lesson 3	Justification by Faith *Romans 5:1-11* *Romans 12:1-15*	October 15th
Lesson 4	Christian Living *Romans 12:1*	October 22nd
Lesson 5	Comments on the Golden Text *I Corinthians 8:1-13*	October 29th
Lesson 6	Science of the Christ Principle *I Corinthians 12:1-26*	November 5th
Lesson 7	The Grace of Liberality *II Corinthians 8:1-12*	November 12th
Lesson 8	Imitation of Christ *Ephesians 4:20-32*	November 19th
Lesson 9	The Christian Home *Colossians 3:12-25*	November 26th
Lesson 10	*Grateful Obedience* *James 1:16-27*	December 3rd
Lesson 11	The Heavenly Inheritance *I Peter 1:1-12*	December 10th
Lesson 12	The Glorified Saviour *Revelation 1:9-20*	December 17th
Lesson 13	A Christmas Lesson Matthew 2:1-11	December 24th
Lesson 14	Review	December 31st

Eleventh Series

January 1 – March 25, 1894

Lesson 1	The First Adam *Genesis 1:26-31 & 2:1-3*	January 7th
Lesson 2	Adam's Sin and God's Grace *Genesis 3:1-15*	January 14th
Lesson 3	Cain and Abel *Genesis 4:3-13*	January 21st
Lesson 4	God's Covenant With Noah *Genesis 9:8-17*	January 28th
Lesson 5	Beginning of the Hebrew Nation *Genesis 12:1-9*	February 4th
Lesson 6	God's Covenant With Abram *Genesis 17:1-9*	February 11th
Lesson 7	God's Judgment of Sodom *Genesis 18:22-23*	February 18th
Lesson 8	Trial of Abraham's Faith *Genesis 22:1-13*	February 25th
Lesson 9	Selling the Birthright *Genesis 25:27-34*	March 4th
Lesson 10	Jacob at Bethel *Genesis 28:10-22*	March 11th
Lesson 11	Temperance *Proverbs 20:1-7*	March 18th
Lesson 12	Review and Easter *Mark 16:1-8*	March 25th

Twelfth Series

April 1 – June 24, 1894

Lesson 1	Jacob's Prevailing Prayer *Genesis 24:30, 32:9-12*	April 8th
Lesson 2	Discord in Jacob's Family *Genesis 37:1-11*	April 1st
Lesson 3	Joseph Sold into Egypt *Genesis 37:23-36*	April 15th
Lesson 4	Object Lesson in Genesis *Genesis 41:38-48*	April 22nd
Lesson 5	"With Thee is Fullness of Joy" *Genesis 45:1-15*	April 29th
Lesson 6	Change of Heart *Genesis 50:14-26*	May 6th
Lesson 7	Israel in Egypt *Exodus 1:1-14*	May 13th
Lesson 8	The Childhood of Moses *Exodus 2:1-10*	May 20th
Lesson 9	Moses Sent As A Deliverer *Exodus 3:10-20*	May 27th
Lesson 10	The Passover Instituted *Exodus 12:1-14*	June 3rd
Lesson 11	Passage of the Red Sea *Exodus 14:19-29*	June 10th
Lesson 12	The Woes of the Drunkard *Proverbs 23:29-35*	June 17th
Lesson 13	Review	June 24th

Thirteenth Series

July 1 – September 30, 1894

Lesson 1	The Birth of Jesus *Luke 2:1-16*	July 1st
Lesson 2	Presentation in the Temple *Luke 2:25-38*	July 8th
Lesson 3	Visit of the Wise Men *Matthew 1:2-12*	July 15th
Lesson 4	Flight Into Egypt *Mathew 2:13-23*	July 22nd
Lesson 5	The Youth of Jesus *Luke2:40-52*	July 29th
Lesson 6	The "All is God" Doctrine *Luke 2:40-52*	August 5th
Lesson 7	Missing	August 12th
Lesson 8	First Disciples of Jesus *John 1:36-49*	August 19th
Lesson 9	The First Miracle of Jesus *John 2:1-11*	August 26th
Lesson 10	Jesus Cleansing the Temple *John 2:13-25*	September 2nd
Lesson 11	Jesus and Nicodemus *John 3:1-16*	September 9th
Lesson 12	Jesus at Jacob's Well *John 4:9-26*	September 16th
Lesson 13	Daniel's Abstinence *Daniel 1:8-20*	September 23rd
Lesson 14	Review *John 2:13-25*	September 30th

Fourteenth Series

October 7 – December 30, 1894

Lesson 1	Jesus At Nazareth *Luke 4:16-30*	October 7th
Lesson 2	The Draught of Fishes *Luke 5:1-11*	October 14th
Lesson 3	The Sabbath in Capernaum *Mark 1:21-34*	October 21st
Lesson 4	The Paralytic Healed *Mark 2:1-12*	October 28th
Lesson 5	Reading of Sacred Books *Mark 2:23-38, Mark 3:1-5*	November 4th
Lesson 6	Spiritual Executiveness *Mark 3:6-19*	November 11th
Lesson 7	Twelve Powers Of The Soul *Luke 6:20-31*	November 18th
Lesson 8	Things Not Understood Attributed to Satan *Mark 3:22-35*	November 25th
Lesson 9	Independence of Mind *Luke 7:24-35*	December 2nd
Lesson 10	The Gift of Untaught Wisdom *Luke 8:4-15*	December 9th
Lesson 11	The Divine Eye Within *Matthew 5:5-16*	December 16th
Lesson 12	Unto Us a Child I s Born *Luke 7:24-35*	December 23rd
Lesson 13	Review *Isaiah 9:2-7*	December 30th

Fifteenth Series

January 6-March 31, 1895

Lesson 1	Missing *Mark 6:17-29*	January 6th
Lesson 2	The Prince Of The World *Mark 6:30-44*	January 13th
Lesson 3	The Golden Text *John 6:25-35*	January 20th
Lesson 4	The Golden Text *Matthew 16:13-25*	January 27th
Lesson 5	The Transfiguration Luke 9:28-36	February 3rd
Lesson 6	Christ And The Children *Matthew 18:1-14*	February 10th
Lesson 7	The Good Samaritan *Luke 10:25-37*	February 17th
Lesson 8	Christ And The Man Born Blind *John 9:1-11*	February 24th
Lesson 9	The Raising Of Lazarus *John 11:30-45*	March 3rd
Lesson 10	The Rich Young Ruler *Mark 10:17-27*	March 10th
Lesson 11	Zaccheus The Publican *Luke 1:10*	March 17th
Lesson 12	Purity Of Life Romans 13:8-14	March 24th
Lesson 13	Review	March 31st

Sixteenth Series

April 7-June 30, 1895

Lesson 1	The Triumphal Entry *Mark 11:1-11*	April 7th
Lesson 2	The Easter Lesson *Mark 12:1-12*	April 14th
Lesson 3	Watchfulness Mark 24:42-51	April 21st
Lesson 4	The Lord's Supper *Mark 14:12-26*	April 28th
Lesson 5	Jesus in Gethsemane Mark 15:42-52	May 5th
Lesson 6	The Jesus Christ Power *Mark 14:53-72*	May 12th
Lesson 7	Jesus Before Pilate *Mark 15:1-15*	May 19th
Lesson 8	The Day of the Crucifixion *Mark 15:22-37*	May 26th
Lesson 9	At the Tomb *Mark 16:1-8*	June 2nd
Lesson 10	The Road To Emmaus *Luke 24:13-32*	June 9th
Lesson 11	Fisher of Men *John 21:4-17*	June 16th
Lesson 12	Missing Luke 24:27-29	June 23rd
Lesson 13	Review	June 30th

Seventeenth Series

July 7 – September 29, 1895

Lesson 1	The Bread of Energy *Exodus 22:1-17*	July 7th
Lesson 2	Grandeur is Messiahship *Exodus 32:30-35*	July 14th
Lesson 3	Temperance *Leviticus 10:1-9*	July 21st
Lesson 4	The Alluring Heart of Man *Numbers 10:29-36*	July 28th
Lesson 5	As a Man Thinketh Numbers 13:17-23	August 4th
Lesson 6	Rock of Eternal Security *Numbers 31:4-9*	August 11th
Lesson 7	Something Behind *Deuteronomy 6:3-15*	August 18th
Lesson 8	What You See Is What You Get *Joshua 3:5-17*	August 25th
Lesson 9	Every Man To His Miracle *Joshua 6:8-20*	September 1st
Lesson 10	Every Man To His Harvest *Joshua 14:5-14*	September 8th
Lesson 11	Every Man To His Refuge *Joshua 20:1-9*	September 15th
Lesson 12	The Twelve Propositions Joshua 24:14-25	September 22nd
Lesson 13	Review I Kings 8:56	September 29th

www.ingramcontent.com/pod-product-compliance
Lightning Source LLC
Chambersburg PA
CBHW062227080426
42734CB00010B/2056